KNOW THE

Secret

To Nurture your Inner Mathematician

Laxmi Mittal

ABOUT THE AUTHOR

 **Laxmi Mittal**, a highly experienced post-graduate teacher in Mathematics, has dedicated 22 years of her life to the noble profession of teaching. Throughout her rich and extensive career, she has keenly observed that many students tend to view Mathematics more as an obligation rather than an area of genuine interest and exploration. This realization, despite the universal and profound nature of Mathematics as a language, prompted her to delve deeper into understanding this common issue.

Recognizing the challenges that students face in embracing Mathematics, Laxmi engaged in a process of thorough introspection and extensive brainstorming. This thoughtful reflection ultimately gave rise to a groundbreaking idea – the development of a comprehensive book specifically tailored to address the anxiety and discomfort that many students experience when engaging with Mathematics.

Laxmi's ultimate goal is to not only empower young learners, but also to support teachers, parents, and professionals with the tools and resources needed to alleviate their anxieties and cultivate a positive and enriching relationship with Mathematics, both academically and professionally. Her vision is to revolutionize the approach to learning and teaching Mathematics, fostering a deep and enduring appreciation for this beautiful language and its practical applications.

DEDICATION

This book is dedicated to my Loving Father Late Sh. Radhey Shyam Kansal

And

This book is dedicated to you.

*"You will live in a different reality, a different life, and people will look at you and say, 'What do you do differently from me?' Well, the only thing that is the difference is that you work with **The Secret**."*

ACKNOWLEDGEMENT

I am filled with profound gratitude as I express my appreciation for Dr Manjunath MS, whose unwavering motivation, support, and guidance have played a pivotal role in turning a mere desire and idea into the reality of this book. His mentorship has been nothing short of a divine blessing.

I deeply bow in reverence to my Master Choa Kok Sui, whose continuous flow of wisdom, ideas, and guidance has been instrumental in shaping the content of this book. "Thank you, Master! Thank you, Master! Thank you, Master!"

My heartfelt thanks go to my guru, Ms. Lakshmy Dhevi, whose invaluable teachings have sown the seeds of the thoughts and aspirations in my heart, which have blossomed into the pages of this book.

I extend my heartfelt appreciation to my son, Pulkit Mittal, whose love, support, and vital contributions have been instrumental in transforming the manuscript into the masterpiece that it is, ensuring its legacy for future generations.

I am deeply grateful to Swatee Sadhana Singh for her role in alleviating the burdens of my childhood and for giving wings to my profound aspirations.

Special thanks to Sooraj Achar for providing unparalleled support in bringing this book to the world.

I also extend my gratitude to the mathematics community for their unwavering support.

I am thankful to Mr. A.K. Sharma and Mrs. Pratibha Sharma for providing the platform for the seedling of my desire.

I express my gratitude to Mr. B.B. Gupta and Dr Neeru Joshi, who have extended their guiding hands to lift me at the beginning of my career.

My heartfelt love and gratitude go to my dear brothers, Mr Brij Mohan and Mr Tarun Kansal, as well as my husband, Mr Alok Kumar Mittal, for their unwavering support.

I express my love and utmost gratitude to my mother, without whose unwavering support, this book would not have come into existence.

Finally, I am grateful to all my mentors and individuals who have crossed my path throughout my life, as their support has been instrumental in my continuous learning and growth.

Laxmi Mittal

FOREWORD

It gives me immense pleasure to write the foreword for Laxmi Mittal's book, "Know the Secret". In today's fast-paced and competitive world, students face immense pressure not only from academic studies but also from the high expectations of their parents and teachers. It's not just students who struggle; parents, teachers, and professionals from all walks of life are also striving for success and fulfillment.

As a principal, motivational speaker, counselor, and mathematics teacher, I have witnessed firsthand the challenges students encounter when dealing with mathematics. Whether it's the complexity of the subject matter, anxiety, fear of competition, or other obstacles, many students struggle to achieve their desired results. In "Know the Secret", Laxmi Mittal shares valuable tools to help students realize their true potential and uncover the universal truth that they possess inherent strength and abilities.

It is heartening to note that her immense knowledge and experience in teaching has been distilled to bring out valuable pearls of wisdom,compiled in the form of this book which is easy to understand and practice for a positive vibrant life.

One of the distinguishing features of this book is its comprehensive approach to personal, academic, and professional growth. Laxmi Mittal recognizes that students must first understand their thoughts and beliefs to unlock their full potential. The book offers practical and actionable strategies that readers can immediately implement in their lives.

"Know the Secret" promotes the importance of forgiveness, gratitude, and affirmations as universal keys to self-discovery. As a principal, I wholeheartedly recommend this book to students, as it introduces powerful tools that can aid in their personal development. The book also provides a simple framework for cultivating self-discipline which is needed every hour.

With its 12 insightful chapters, including "The Power of Belief" and "Know Who You Are", the book empowers readers to face challenges with confidence and develop resilience. I am confident that "Know the Secret" will serve as a valuable resource for academic, personal, and professional growth, providing readers with a competitive edge in today's rapidly evolving world.

I extend my heartfelt congratulations to Laxmi Mittal for crafting this insightful and invaluable book. I am certain that "Know the Secret" will inspire readers to break through barriers and embark on a remarkable journey of growth. Let us come together to unleash the full potential that lies within each of us.

Dr NEERU JOSHI
Principal
Global speaker, Counsellor,
Motivator, NLP Expert
Mental health and wellness Coach

PRAISE FOR
"KNOW THE SECRET"

Stunning and Amazing. "Know the secret - Nurture Your Inner Mathematician" is a transformative book that introduces mindful strategies to alleviate the mental fears and phobias that hinder students' potential to learn and understand mathematics. By emphasizing analysis and application, this book empowers readers to unleash their potential, transforming weakness, fear, and anxiety into courage and confidence. It's a must-read for all students seeking to overcome their challenges and excel in mathematics.

UMA GUPTA

Author of the Book " The wellness code for vibrant aging"

"Know the Secret" by Laxmi Mittal offers a comprehensive and holistic approach to empowerment, guiding students, educators, and parents in discovering and unlocking their inner potential. Addressing the pressing need of our times, this book is an essential read for anyone seeking personal and academic growth.

Mayank J Kanabar
Author of the Book "Know, Own & Awaken the Hero within you"

CONTENTS

INTRODUCTION

For the past 22 years, I have dedicated my life to teaching. I am a Post Graduate Teacher (PGT) in Mathematics. Throughout my career, I have observed that many students seem to choose Mathematics not out of genuine interest, but rather out of a sense of obligation. As a result, they face challenges in understanding the subject matter and struggle academically.

Recognizing this common issue, I delved into a deep process of introspection and brainstorming. This thoughtful reflection ultimately led to the inception of a groundbreaking idea - developing a comprehensive book tailored to address the anxiety and discomfort experienced by students when it comes to Mathematics. My goal is to equip young learners with the tools and resources needed to ease their apprehensions and foster a positive relationship not only with math, but with their academic and professional growth.

I am deeply grateful to Mrs. Rhonda Byrne, Mr. Charles Francis Haanel, Dr. Carol Susan Dweck, Mr. Robin Sharma, and Mr. Stephen Covey. Their influence has played a pivotal role in shaping

the trajectory of this initiative, which aims to empower the upcoming generations.

Laxmi Mittal

CHAPTER 1

THOUGHTS - THE POWERFUL MAGNETS

"What we think, we become"

– Buddha

Throughout history, people have always liked to be around other people and form connections with them. These connections can be with family, friends, or colleagues, and they are important for making us feel like we belong and for our overall happiness.

Also, what a lot of people believe together can have a big effect on all of us. When many people share a particular belief, it can become even more important to all of us, making it have a bigger impact on our lives.

Over time, as we repeatedly hear the same statement, it gains power in our subconscious mind. Eventually, it becomes ingrained in our beliefs.

When someone tells us that pizza is delicious, we often trust their opinion. It's possible that the first bite might not immediately appeal to our taste buds, but as we continue to savour it, our perception of its flavour may change, and we may find ourselves enjoying it more with each bite.

If you want material things like a watch or a laptop, your mind sends out these frequencies to the universe. As a result, you attract the things you want. This is called the **"Law of Attraction".** When you think, your thoughts are sent out into the universe and attract similar thoughts. Charles Haanel explained that thoughts act like magnets, pulling in other thoughts that are on the same frequency.

We can see pictures on our TV screens because transmission towers broadcast specific frequencies and convert them into images. Using the remote control, we can change the frequencies and switch between different channels to view various pictures on the TV screen from the comfort of our couch.

Did you know that you are like a powerful transmission tower? You have the incredible ability to transmit energy and vibrations that can reach far beyond the borders of our world.

Your transmission has the power to shape your life and your surroundings. It's like you're broadcasting your frequency to the entire Universe. For example, when you remember your mother, she may pick up on the signals and realise you are missing her, even if she is far away.

One strong perception in our society is that Math is really difficult. Your lack of math skills is being reflected in you through the frequency of your thoughts. Every day, you may catch yourself thinking, "I can't do Math. It's so logical and requires heaps of practice. Math isn't my thing. I feel like my brain isn't wired for it. Even with all the practice, I still struggle to score well. My parents have pressured me into choosing this because Sharma's son is also choosing the same. This is crucial for pursuing higher studies... etc."

Let's comprehend the influence of constructive thoughts through a real-life narrative. In the 1960s, Norman Cousins, an American journalist, author, and professor, received a life-changing diagnosis of ankylosing spondylitis, a rare and excruciating disease that primarily affects the spine. Despite being given a bleak prognosis with a short time left to live, he refused to succumb to despair. Instead, he took matters into his own hands by embracing an unconventional approach based on the power of positivity and the mind-body connection.

Choosing to leave the hospital, Cousins opted for a hotel room where he surrounded himself with laughter and positivity. He dedicated himself to watching comedic movies, reading humorous literature, and engaging in activities that brought him joy. His firm belief in the ability of laughter and a positive mindset to alleviate pain and contribute to healing guided his unconventional treatment plan.

Extraordinarily, Cousins' condition began to improve, with his pain diminishing significantly and his health gradually returning. His remarkable recovery confounded medical professionals and stood as a testament to the remarkable capacity of the human mind. Subsequently, Cousins penned "Anatomy of an Illness," chronicling his journey and emphasising the pivotal role of positive thoughts and laughter in his healing process.

This remarkable account underscores the profound impact of our thoughts on our physical well-being. Norman Cousins' resilience and commitment to positivity showcase the immense potential of the mind in overcoming severe illness and regaining health, solidifying the notion that the mind indeed wields profound influence.

It's important to remember that farmers yield the crop of the seedlings they plant. For instance, if they sow mango seeds, they will eventually harvest mangoes. Similarly, if they plant apple seeds, they will reap apples when the crop matures.

This analogy can be applied to our thoughts as well. Our thoughts can be compared to seeds, and just like seeds, our thoughts also yield results. If we constantly dwell on fearful thoughts, we'll likely experience increased anxiety and fearfulness. On the other hand, if we focus on positive thoughts, we can expect to see more positivity in our lives.

Therefore, if we wish to bring about change in our lives, we must alter our thought patterns. This can be achieved by intentionally changing our mindset and focusing on positive thoughts. By doing so, we can elevate our vibrational frequency and create a more positive and fulfilling life for ourselves.

5 Key Takeaways: Thoughts - The Powerful Magnets

1. Power of Beliefs: Shared beliefs can significantly impact our lives and society.

2. Law of Attraction: Our thoughts attract similar energy from the universe, influencing our experiences.

3. Transmission of Thoughts: Like a transmission tower, our thoughts can reach and affect others.

4. Mind-Body Connection: Positive thinking can lead to remarkable physical healing, as shown by Norman Cousins.

5. Thoughts as Seeds: Our thoughts shape our reality; focusing on positive thoughts brings positive outcomes.

CHAPTER 2

UNDERSTANDING THE "MATH MINDSET"

"No one can make you feel inferior without your consent"

- Eleanor Roosevelt

Why do many students find mathematics challenging?

The answer to this question lies in the "Math Mindset." Our perceptions and attitudes towards Mathematics significantly influence our ability to comprehend and excel in the subject. This suggests that our thoughts and beliefs about Mathematics play a crucial role in determining our success in learning and applying Mathematical concepts.

The life story of Thomas Alva Edison is a remarkable example of resilience and the transformative power of a growth mindset. Despite facing academic struggles, particularly in Mathematics, during his early years, Edison's innate curiosity and intelligence were evident. However, his difficulties in school, especially in Math, led his teachers to believe he was lazy and incapable of achieving good grades.

Faced with this discouragement, Edison's mother recognized his potential and decided to homeschool him. She nurtured his interest in science and experimentation, providing him with the freedom to explore and discover his aptitude for understanding the inner workings of various phenomena and inventing new technologies.

Though Edison initially grappled with mathematical concepts, his unwavering determination and the support of his mother instilled in him a growth mindset. This newfound perspective enabled him to realize that with persistent effort, he could excel in any endeavour. As a result, he emerged as one of history's most prolific inventors, revolutionising the world with groundbreaking innovations such as the electric light bulb and the phonograph.

Contrary to popular belief, Edison's success was not solely an outcome of solitary experimentation. In reality, he collaborated with a team of thirty assistants and experienced scientists in a state-of-the-art laboratory funded by corporate resources. Their tireless efforts, which often involved round-the-clock work, emphasized the iterative nature of innovation. Each failure served as a stepping stone, propelling them forward to achieve their ultimate objectives.

The enduring lesson from Edison's narrative is a powerful testament to the impact of perseverance and a growth-oriented mindset. His journey illustrates that, regardless of initial challenges, relentless commitment and an adaptable outlook can lead to extraordinary accomplishments.

In the preceding section, we delved into the profound impact of thoughts and attitudes on our Math Mindset. It's essential to recognize that our mindset can be categorized into two types - fixed mindset and growth mindset.

A fixed mindset is characterized by the belief that one's math ability is unchangeable. Individuals with a fixed mindset tend to avoid challenging math problems out of fear of failure. They may view mistakes as evidence that math is not their strong suit, leading to a persistent sense of inadequacy.

Conversely, a growth mindset embodies the belief that one can improve their math skills through diligent effort and a willingness to learn from mistakes. Those with a growth mindset see challenges as opportunities for growth and development, exhibiting a resilient attitude towards tough math problems.

Students with a growth mindset view mistakes as valuable learning experiences, propelling them to stay motivated and persist in tackling difficult math problems. They understand that struggling with a concept is simply a natural part of the learning process, not an indication of their intelligence.

On the other hand, students with a fixed mindset tend to view their math abilities as fixed traits, leaving no room for improvement. This mindset may lead them to shy away from challenging problems, fearing that failure would be a reflection of their intelligence. As a result, they may miss out on valuable learning opportunities.

Research has shown that students with a growth mindset perform better in math and excel in various areas of their lives. Believing in their capacity for improvement, they demonstrate greater perseverance, resilience, and enjoyment of math as they gradually enhance their skills over time.

Understanding the math mindset involves acknowledging that our belief in our potential for improvement significantly influences our learning experience and attitude towards the subject. Cultivating a growth mindset empowers individuals to develop greater proficiency and confidence in math, benefiting their academic endeavours and their broader approach to learning and problem-solving.

5 Key Takeaways: Understanding the "Math Mindset"

1. Math Mindset: Beliefs about math ability impact comprehension and success.

2. Edison's Resilience: Overcoming academic struggles through a growth mindset led to groundbreaking inventions.

3. Fixed vs. Growth Mindset: Fixed mindset limits potential; growth mindset encourages improvement.

4. Perseverance: Persistent effort and learning from mistakes enhance math skills and overall learning.

5. Research Findings: Students with a growth mindset perform better and enjoy learning more.

Chapter 3

THE POWER OF BELIEF

*"Don't be pushed by the fears in your mind, be led by
the dreams in your heart"*

– Roy T. Bennett

Believing in oneself is crucial for developing a growth mindset and approaching math problems with confidence. This idea, referred to as the "power of belief," involves maintaining a positive mindset and trusting that improvement comes from effort, practice, and the understanding that intelligence can be developed through hard work and dedication, rather than being fixed traits that we are born with.

Through positive belief, it is possible to rewire the brain.

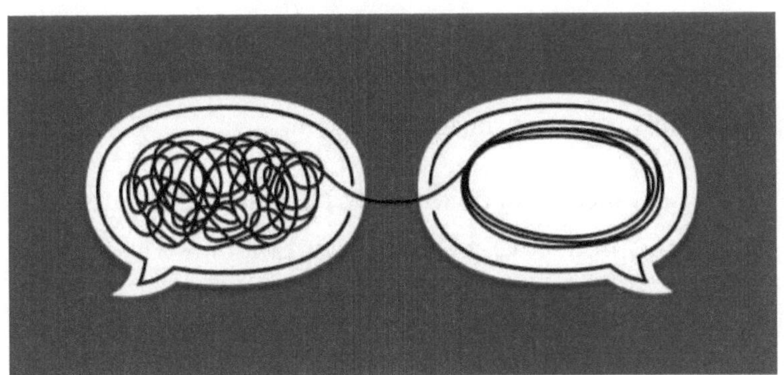

I recently came across an interesting explanation about why the majority of people do not experience their greatness and why only a small percentage of individuals are truly creative and productive. According to the Triune Brain Model, our brain is divided into three parts: the ancient brain, the limbic system, and the prefrontal cortex.

The ancient brain, which is negativity-biased, tends to prioritize and capture negativity. As our brains evolved, from the ancient brain to the limbic system and then to the prefrontal cortex, emotions began to play a significant role in our daily lives. We tend to feel happy when we are in our comfort zone, but the moment we contemplate stepping out of it, fear becomes the primary emotion at play. The amygdala, an almond-shaped structure in the limbic brain, detects fear and becomes activated.

When we aspire to dream bigger, learn faster, and elevate our levels of creativity and productivity, a conflict arises between the ancient brain and the mastery brain, leading to a sort of internal war. The ancient brain recognizes our growth and perceives that we are moving away from our safe zone, triggering the release of the fear hormone cortisol. Consequently, we begin to undermine the creative aspects of the mastery brain.

This insight sheds light on why only 1% of individuals are highly creative and productive - because they are the ones willing to face and battle through these internal conflicts.

Improving your confidence in solving math problems is essential for success in mathematics. Here are some detailed tips to help you enhance your belief in yourself:

1. *Practice Regularly:* Regular practice is crucial for improving your math skills. Make a habit of practising math problems daily to build your confidence and proficiency. The more you practice, the more comfortable and confident you'll become with math concepts and problem-solving techniques.

2. *Embrace Mistakes:* Instead of fearing mistakes, consider them as stepping stones to learning. Every mistake is an opportunity to identify areas that need improvement. Learn from your mistakes, analyse why they occurred, and use them as valuable learning experiences to enhance your problem-solving abilities.

3. *Set Small Goals:* Tackling big math problems can be overwhelming. Break them down into smaller, more manageable steps. Setting achievable goals for each step and celebrating your progress along the way will help build your confidence and motivation.

4. *Use Positive Self-Talk:* Your mindset plays a significant role in problem-solving. Replace negative self-talk with positive affirmations. Instead of thinking, "I can't do this," tell yourself, "I can learn this with effort and practice." Positive self-talk can shift your perspective and boost your confidence when facing challenging math problems.

5. *Ask for Help:* Seeking assistance is a sign of strength, not weakness. If you're stuck on a problem or concept, don't hesitate to ask for help. Approach your teacher, a knowledgeable friend, or a parent for guidance. Explaining where you're struggling can lead to valuable insights and support to overcome obstacles.

6. *Work with Peers:* Studying with friends or classmates can be a powerful way to reinforce your understanding of math concepts. Teaching and explaining concepts to others can solidify your comprehension while also providing an opportunity to learn from your peers. Collaborative learning environments can strengthen your problem-solving skills and confidence in math.

7. *Seek career guidance*: Seeking career guidance is an important step towards deciding on a career path that aligns with your interests, skills, and aspirations. Through career guidance, you can gain valuable insights and advice that will assist you in making informed decisions about your future. With the right guidance, you can develop a clear understanding of how learning Math can contribute to your career goals and help you pave a promising path forward. This guidance will not only provide clarity but also instill a positive mindset, boost confidence, and cultivate a resilient attitude that will enable you to overcome obstacles and thrive in the field of Mathematics.

In summary, the power of belief in math is about understanding that with hard work and the right mindset, anyone can improve their math skills. This belief helps students approach math problems with confidence, persistence, and a positive attitude.

5 Key Takeaways: The Power of Belief

1. Power of Belief: Believing in oneself fosters a growth mindset and boosts confidence in math.

2. Brain Dynamics: The ancient brain's fear response hinders creativity and productivity; overcoming this is key.

3. Practice and Perseverance: Regular practice, embracing mistakes, and setting small goals enhance math skills.

4. Positive Self-Talk and Support: Positive affirmations and seeking help build confidence and understanding.

5. Collaborative Learning: Working with peers and seeking career guidance strengthens problem-solving abilities and aligns math skills with career goals.

CHAPTER 4
KNOW WHO YOU ARE

"You, 've come to this juncture in your life, merely because something in you kept saying," You deserve to be happy" You were born to add something, to add value to this world. To simply be something, bigger and better than you were yesterday. Every single thing you have been through, every single moment that you have come through, were to all prepare you for this moment right now. Imagine, what you can do from this day forward with what you now know. Now you get that you are the creator of your destiny. So, how much more do you get to do? how much more do you get to be? how many more people do you get to bless, simply by mere your existence? what will you do with the moment? No one can dance your dance, no one else can sing your song, no one else can write your story. Who you are, what you do, begins, right now!" **- Lisa Nicholls**

I still vividly remember the day I was born. It was a joyous occasion for my parents and family. Being their fourth child, my arrival was celebrated with great enthusiasm. My father had high hopes and aspirations for me, envisioning that I would achieve what he could not. He saw me as the means to fulfil his unmet dreams. On the other hand, my mother wished for me to become a proficient and skilled young woman capable of handling all household duties flawlessly. She believed that these skills were essential to be a good daughter-in-law in the future.

Alongside these expectations, other family members advised against investing too much in my education or skill development, citing the societal belief that it was a waste to invest in a girl child. These societal norms and conditioning shaped my upbringing, and I was unaware of my right to make my own choices. This was true not just for me, but for everyone growing up within these societal constraints.

It wasn't until May 2019, when I attended an inner engineering workshop conducted by Director Sir, Mr AK Sharma at my workplace, Bhai Parmanand Vidya Mandir School, that the first door to self-discovery was opened for me. During the workshop, I discovered my affinity for silence, something I had never truly experienced before. This workshop provided me with the rare opportunity to explore my preferences and choices, a privilege that many people do not have.

I felt blessed to have found inner calmness and guidance, something that 99% of people seem to miss out on due to the internal noise that clouds their perception. It made me realize that just like the impartial nature of the sun, air, and natural resources, the universe offers its blessings equally to all. The only hindrance to receiving them in full measure is our lack of receptivity and self-recognition.

Who are you?

- You are a Divine being and have a divine plan on Earth

- You are unique

- You have unique skill sets

- You have unique strengths

- You have a unique weakness

- You are here for a definite purpose as per the divine plan.

Believe that your life is in perfect balance with nature and that you are here to grow and thrive. To unlock your potential, upgrading your skills and expanding your knowledge is essential. This is why the pursuit of education is so important. Mathematics, as the language of the universe, offers a unique opportunity to unravel the mysteries of the cosmos. Embracing this subject will undoubtedly empower you to discover and create in remarkable ways.

Nature serves as an extraordinary instructor by demonstrating its ability to unfold in a harmonious and precise manner. The changing of seasons, the gradual growth of a tree, and the ebb and flow of the tides all transpire with impeccable timing and order. This inherent perfection in nature can serve as a profound analogy to help us overcome challenges in mathematics. Just as nature's processes lead to growth and mastery, so too can our struggles with math become a natural part of our learning and development.

The Perfection of Nature

Consider the cycle of a plant's growth. It starts as a tiny seed buried in the soil, seemingly insignificant and powerless. However, with the right amount of water, sunlight, and nutrients, it gradually breaks through the ground, growing into a strong, tall plant. This process takes time, patience, and consistent care. Just as the seed needs the right conditions to thrive, students need the right mindset and strategies to excel in Math.

Math as a Natural Process

Understanding and mastering Mathematics is a complex yet rewarding journey that shares similarities with the process of nature. Similar to the growth of a plant, mathematical proficiency also requires time and consistent effort. It's essential to recognise that every small step forward is progress, even if it may not appear evident immediately. Embracing the challenges encountered in mathematics as natural aspects of the learning process is crucial for students.

Growth takes Time: Just as plants face obstacles such as storms and droughts, math problems that seem difficult serve as opportunities for students to strengthen their problem-solving skills and mental resilience. Overcoming these challenges contributes to greater understanding and confidence in tackling complex mathematical concepts.

Patience and Persistence: The patience and persistence demonstrated by a dedicated gardener reflect the mindset essential for approaching mathematics. Regular practice, seeking assistance when required, and persevering through difficulties are crucial habits that lead to proficiency in math.

Finding the Right Conditions: Similar to how plants require specific conditions to thrive, students need the right environment and resources to study mathematics effectively. This includes a quiet and distraction-free study space, access to educational materials, and a positive mindset that fosters a love for learning.

Trusting into Process: Trusting the process of learning, similar to how nature unfolds over time, is vital for students. Even when progress seems gradual, sustained effort and a positive attitude will yield substantial results over time. It's important to celebrate small victories and acknowledge that every bit of effort contributes to overall growth.

Practical Steps for Math Mastery

Consistent and Regular Practice: Just like how a plant needs to be watered consistently, it's important for students to regularly practice their math skills to reinforce and solidify their understanding of mathematical concepts. By setting aside dedicated time for practice, students can improve their proficiency in math.

Seeking Help and Guidance: Similar to how a gardener might consult an expert for advice on how to care for their plants, students should not hesitate to seek help from their teachers, tutors, or online resources when they encounter difficulties with math. Getting guidance and assistance can provide valuable insights and help students overcome any obstacles they may face in their mathematical studies.

Breaking Down Complex Problems: Complex math problems can be challenging to tackle all at once, much like a plant's growth occurs one leaf at a time. By breaking down large math problems into smaller, more manageable parts, students can approach problem-solving in a strategic and organized way, making it easier to understand and solve intricate mathematical problems.

Cultivating a Positive Mindset: Adopting a positive mindset towards math can play a significant role in transforming struggles into opportunities for growth. By viewing challenges as chances to learn and improve, students can build resilience and confidence in their mathematical abilities, leading to a more positive and successful learning experience.

Conclusion

Students need to understand that the natural order of things means that everything in nature occurs perfectly. This perspective can help students view their struggles with math as a normal and essential part of their learning journey. By acknowledging that progress takes time, facing challenges builds resilience, and persistence yields results, students can approach math with the confidence and patience required to succeed. Just as a small seed grows into a mighty tree, each student possesses the potential to conquer their mathematical challenges and excel in the subject, using their difficulties as valuable building blocks on the path to mastery.

5 Key Takeaways: Know Who You Are

1. Believe in Yourself: Confidence and a growth mindset are key to overcoming challenges in math.

2. Inner Strength: Recognize your unique strengths and weaknesses; embrace your purpose.

3. Embrace Learning: Education and skill development are essential for unlocking your potential.

4. Nature's Lessons: Nature's processes teach us patience, persistence, and the importance of the right conditions for growth.

5. Consistent Effort: Regular practice, seeking help, breaking down problems, and maintaining a positive mindset are crucial for mastering math and achieving personal growth.

CHAPTER 5

HOW TO RECOGNISE YOURSELF?

"These three things are especially hard:
Steel, a diamond and to know one's self"

- Benjamin Franklin (1706-1790)

On a bright and pleasant day, Ram set out to the market in search of the perfect gaming station. His excitement knew no bounds when he stumbled upon a high-quality gaming station that met his requirements and fell within his budget. Delighted with his purchase, his parents ensured the device was carefully packed for the journey home. Within mere moments of reaching home, Ram eagerly delved into exploring the gaming station's array of features and functions. Thanks to the well-crafted user manual accompanying the gaming station, he effortlessly familiarised himself with its capabilities.

The experience of acquiring electronic devices often comes with the added benefit of receiving a comprehensive user manual. This manual serves as a guide, offering insights into the product's functionality, usage, and essential do's and don'ts. Despite this invaluable resource for electronic devices, it's intriguing to ponder the absence of a user manual for humanity itself.

The complexity and beauty of human existence make it clear that scientists, no matter how skilled they are, can't recreate the intricate design of a human being. While scientists can create artificial intelligence and robots, making a human being is beyond their abilities. Living as a human involves dealing with the body and circumstances we're born with, adapting to different situations and choices, and understanding the complexities of our existence.

Dear reader, have you ever considered the idea that our physical body consists of two distinct parts? It's true - our body can be thought of as having a left and a right side. Just like a well-functioning vehicle relies on balance, our body also needs to balance these two parts to operate efficiently. However, unlike a vehicle, we don't have a manual that provides insight into how to achieve this balance.

Interestingly, the universe itself can be considered a manual for human existence. Every message we need to live a fulfilling life is transmitted to us through our consciousness. Conceptualise the universe as a transmitter and our consciousness as a receiver, with our breathing serving as the medium through which these messages are transferred. Therefore, everyone needs to be conscious and mindful to make the most of this connection.

Imagine you are driving your vehicle, it may be your bicycle, scooter, or car. Can you drive it smoothly if its tyres are not inflated properly? Maybe one tyre has no air and the other is filled properly. Then, of course, you cannot drive it smoothly. In the same way, our physical body is like a vehicle for our soul. Our soul is the driver of this physical body. Our body gets inflated by our breathing. And, if we are not breathing properly then it cannot be balanced.

When we don't breathe properly, the balance between the left and right parts of our body is disrupted, leading to feelings of anger, frustration, and anxiety. That's why it's important to make a conscious effort to balance our breathing regularly. This practice only requires a maximum of 15 minutes out of the 1440 minutes in a day.

In the modern, fast-paced world, adolescents often encounter significant academic stress and numerous distractions that can impact their cognitive abilities, particularly memory retention. One often underappreciated but highly effective approach to improving memory is balanced breathing. Balanced breathing encompasses techniques such as diaphragmatic breathing, alternate nostril breathing, and box breathing. These practices have been shown to have a substantial positive impact on cognitive functions and can contribute to improved overall mental well-being.

Benefits of Balanced Breathing

Enhanced Oxygen Supply to the Brain: Utilizing balanced breathing techniques, such as deep diaphragmatic breathing, ensures consistent and optimal delivery of oxygen to the brain. This heightened oxygenation not only enhances brain function but also contributes to improved memory retention and recall. The brain, as a highly metabolically active organ, relies on a consistent and efficient oxygen supply to operate at its best.

Stress Reduction: Prolonged exposure to stress can have detrimental effects on memory by causing the hippocampus, the brain region responsible for creating new memories, to shrink. Balanced breathing techniques, such as diaphragmatic breathing and box breathing, activate the parasympathetic nervous system, leading to a relaxation response that reduces stress. This calming effect helps safeguard the hippocampus from stress-induced damage, thereby bolstering memory function.

Improved Concentration and Focus: Techniques like alternate nostril breathing can enhance concentration and focus by harmonizing the activity between the brain's two hemispheres. Heightened focus directly contributes to improved memory, as individuals can more effectively process and recall information when they are less susceptible to distractions.

Regulation of Emotions: Balanced breathing aids in emotional regulation by influencing the autonomic nervous system. Managing emotions is vital for memory function, as elevated levels of anxiety or depression can impair cognitive abilities. By promoting emotional stability, balanced breathing assists in maintaining an optimal mental state for learning and memory retention.

Types of Balanced Breathing

1. *Rhythmic Abdominal Breathing*, also known as Diaphragmatic Breathing, is a technique that involves taking slow, deep breaths to maximize oxygen intake and induce a sense of calm and relaxation. It is beneficial for overall well-being and has a positive impact on memory consolidation. Here's how to practice it:

1. Find a comfortable seated or lying position.

2. Place one hand on your chest and the other on your abdomen to focus your attention on your breathing.

3. Inhale deeply through your nose, allowing your abdomen to expand while keeping your chest relatively still.

4. Exhale slowly through your mouth, letting your abdomen contract.

5. Maintain a steady, rhythmic pattern of breathing.

*Scan the QR Code
for Rhythmic Abdominal
Breathing*

Practicing rhythmic abdominal breathing offers a variety of benefits, including:

- Reducing stress and anxiety

- Enhancing relaxation and focus

- Improving oxygen exchange in the body

- Lowering blood pressure

- Promoting better sleep

Incorporating this breathing technique into your daily routine can have a positive impact on your overall health and well-being.

2. One effective yogic breathing technique that can help balance the breath and promote calmness and mental clarity is ***Alternate Nostril Breathing***, also known as Nadi Shodhana. This technique involves breathing through one nostril at a time and can be done by following these steps:

1. Find a comfortable seated position with a straight spine.

2. Close your right nostril using your right thumb.

3. Inhale slowly and deeply through your left nostril.

4. Close your left nostril with your right ring finger and release your right nostril.

5. Exhale slowly and completely through your right nostril.

6. Inhale deeply through your right nostril.

7. Close your right nostril and release your left nostril.

8. Exhale slowly and completely through your left nostril.

Practicing this technique is believed to offer several benefits, including:

- Reducing stress and anxiety

- Enhancing concentration and focus

- Balancing the nervous system

- Improving respiratory function

- Promoting overall well-being

3. *Box Breathing*, also known as Square Breathing, is a structured breathing technique designed to promote relaxation and reduce stress and anxiety. Here's how to practice it:

1. Find a comfortable seated position with a straight spine. Close your eyes if it helps you to relax.

2. Inhale deeply and slowly through your nose, counting to 4 as you fill your lungs with air.

3. Hold your breath for a count of 4.

4. Slowly exhale through your mouth for a count of 4, releasing all the air from your lungs.

5. Hold your breath again for a count of 4.

6. Repeat the cycle for several minutes, maintaining a steady and relaxed breathing rhythm.

Practicing this technique is believed to offer several benefits, including:

- Reducing stress and anxiety

- Enhancing concentration and focus

- Promoting relaxation

- Improving respiratory function.

The benefits of practicing Box Breathing include reducing stress and anxiety, enhancing focus and concentration, promoting relaxation, lowering blood pressure, and improving lung capacity and respiratory efficiency. It's a simple yet powerful technique that can be practiced anywhere, anytime to help you find calm and balance in your day.

Potential Risks Involved

While balanced breathing techniques are generally safe and beneficial, there are a few considerations to keep in mind.

It's important to be mindful of potential side effects when starting deep breathing practices, especially if you're new to it. Beginners may experience dizziness or light-headedness, especially if they breathe too quickly or hyperventilate. It's crucial to begin slowly and gradually increase the intensity to minimize these effects.

Additionally, individuals with asthma or other respiratory conditions should seek advice from a healthcare professional before attempting new breathing exercises. Some techniques may need to be adapted to prevent any worsening of their condition.

Furthermore, it's essential to practice balanced breathing under proper guidance to ensure that the techniques are effective and comfortable. Learning from a trained instructor can help in performing the techniques correctly and safely.

Cognitive Benefits of Balanced Breathing

Research on the impact of conscious breathing on cognitive improvement has been gaining traction in recent years, shedding light on how such practices can enhance various cognitive functions, including memory, attention, and emotional regulation. Here are a few key studies and findings:

1. *Yoga and Meditation in Older Adults:* This study, published in the Journal of Alzheimer's Disease, investigated how yoga and meditation, which often involve conscious breathing techniques, affect cognitive functioning in older adults. The researchers observed significant improvements in verbal memory and visuospatial memory among participants. These findings suggest that practices like yoga and meditation, which include conscious breathing, can enhance cognitive functions crucial for both older adults and teenagers.

2. *Breath-Focused Meditation and Emotional Regulation:* Published in the journal Emotion, this study explored how breath-focused meditation influences emotional regulation. Participants who practised this form of meditation showed enhanced emotional regulation and lower stress levels. Because high stress and poor emotional regulation can negatively impact cognitive functions such as memory, these results imply that breath-focused meditation indirectly boosts cognitive performance by promoting better emotional health.

3. *Biological Mechanisms of Controlled Breathing:* Research in the journal Frontiers in Human Neuroscience delved into the biological mechanisms underlying controlled breathing practices. It highlighted that controlled breathing can improve autonomic nervous system function, decrease sympathetic nervous system activity (associated with stress response), and increase parasympathetic activity (associated with relaxation). These physiological changes contribute to improved focus, reduced anxiety, and enhanced cognitive performance, including memory.

4. *Impact of Pranayama on Cognitive Functions:* Pranayama, a practice in yoga involving controlled breathing techniques, was examined in a study published in the International Journal of Yoga. Regular practice of pranayama was found to enhance attention, processing speed, and executive functions. These cognitive enhancements are critical for academic performance in teenagers, suggesting that incorporating pranayama into routines could benefit cognitive abilities.

5. *Breathing-Based Meditation and Cortical Thickness:* A study in Psychiatry Research: Neuroimaging explored how practitioners of breathing-based meditation exhibit increased cortical thickness in brain regions associated with attention and sensory processing. Increased cortical thickness is often linked to better cognitive functions, such as memory and attention. This finding suggests that regular practice of conscious breathing may lead to structural changes in the brain that support improved cognitive abilities.

Overall, these studies collectively indicate that conscious breathing practices have significant benefits for cognitive functions. They enhance brain oxygenation, reduce stress, improve emotional regulation, and may even lead to structural brain changes that support better memory and attention. Integrating conscious breathing exercises into daily routines could therefore be an effective strategy for enhancing cognitive performance, particularly in teenage students who are developing crucial cognitive skills.

5 Key Takeaways: How to Recognise Yourself?

1. Human Complexity: Unlike electronic devices, there is no user manual for understanding human existence, reflecting its profound complexity.

2. Balancing Body and Mind: Like a vehicle requires balanced tires, our body needs balanced breathing for mental and physical harmony.

3. Breathing Techniques: Practices such as diaphragmatic, alternate nostril, and box breathing can enhance cognitive functions and reduce stress.

4. Emotional Regulation: Balanced breathing helps manage emotions, improving overall mental well-being and memory retention.

5. Research Backing: Studies show that conscious breathing techniques improve brain oxygenation, reduce anxiety, and enhance cognitive performance.

CHAPTER 6

POWER OF THE PRESENT MOMENT

P lease take a moment to pause and reflect on the following: How often do you find yourself truly living in the present moment throughout the day? It's common to spend a significant amount of time either dwelling on the past or anticipating the future.

Your mind may often construct narratives and stories that keep you preoccupied, while your body operates on autopilot, carrying out daily tasks. It's possible that you might not even realize that your mind has a strong hold over you, essentially making you a slave to its whims.

Still not convinced? Let's try a simple exercise.

Take a minute to close your eyes and take a few deep breaths. As you do so, simply observe the mental images that come to mind. After a minute, open your eyes and carefully assess the nature of these mental pictures. Are they related to past experiences or future aspirations?

This exercise demonstrates how your physical body may be engaged in routine actions while your mind is elsewhere, focused on something entirely different.

Now, here's a story meant to help you visualize your predicament and suggest ways to overcome this challenge.

Sophia sat at her desk, staring at the screen. The math homework on her laptop seemed to blur together, a confusing mess of numbers and symbols. She sighed, glancing at her phone every few minutes. Social media notifications and messages from friends were far more appealing than quadratic equations. The constant buzzing and flashing of the screen drew her attention away from the homework that seemed impossible to complete.

Her mother, noticing her struggle, walked into the room. "Having trouble, Sophia?"

"Yeah, Mom. Math is impossible. I don't get why I need to learn this stuff anyway."

Her mom smiled and sat down on the edge of the bed. "I used to think the same way. But I learned a trick that might help you. Mind if I share it?"

Sophia shrugged. "Sure, why not."

Her mother pulled up a chair. "It's called living in the present moment. When you focus entirely on what you're doing right now, things start to make sense. Want to give it a try?"

Sophia raised an eyebrow. "Is this like meditation or something?"

"In a way, yes. It's about focusing your mind on the task at hand. Let's do it together. Close your eyes and take a deep breath."

Feeling a bit silly, Sophia closed her eyes and breathed deeply. Her mother continued, "Feel the air as it enters your lungs. Let go of everything else—your phone, your friends, everything. Just be here, right now."

After a few moments, Sophia felt a strange sense of calm. "Now," her mom said, "open your eyes and look at the problem in front of you. Just this one problem, nothing else."

Sophia opened her eyes. The math problem didn't seem as daunting. She took another deep breath and started working through the first step. To her surprise, it made sense. Then the next step and the next, until she solved it.

"Wow," Sophia said, looking up. "That worked."

Her mom smiled. "Living in the present moment helps clear the clutter from your mind. It's like turning off all the distractions so you can focus on what matters."

The next day at school, Sophia's English teacher, Ms. Alvarez, introduced a new reading assignment. The class groaned, but Sophia decided to try her mom's trick again. She closed her eyes, took a deep breath, and focused on the passage in front of her. As she read, she found herself understanding the text more easily, picking up on details she would have missed before.

During lunch, Sophia shared her new approach with her friends. "Guys, you won't believe it, but focusing on the present moment makes homework so much easier."

Her friend Alex looked sceptical. "Seriously? How does that work?"

Sophia explained, "It's like this: when you're doing math or reading, don't think about how hard it is or what else you could be doing. Just focus on the numbers or the words in front of you. Take a deep breath and be here, right now."

Her friends decided to try it, and over the next few weeks, they noticed a difference. Math problems became less confusing, and reading assignments seemed less tedious. They even started a small study group, reminding each other to live in the present moment.

Sophia's phone buzzed again, but this time, she ignored it, diving into her math problems. As she solved each one, she felt a growing sense of accomplishment. It was as if each correct answer was a seed planted in her confidence garden, growing stronger with each step.

One weekend, Sophia and her friends decided to hang out at the park. They spread out a blanket, surrounded by their phones and snacks, ready to relax and chat. However, Sophia couldn't shake the feeling that they were missing something.

"Hey, guys," she said, looking around at the lush greenery. "Have you ever noticed how everything in nature is so focused on the present moment?"

Her friend Emma looked up from her phone. "What do you mean?"

Sophia pointed to a nearby tree. "Look at that tree. It's not worried about what happened yesterday or what's going to happen tomorrow. It's just growing, doing its thing, right now."

Alex laughed. "Sophia, you're starting to sound like a motivational speaker."

"I'm serious," Sophia insisted. "Think about it. When we're constantly distracted by our phones and everything else, we're missing out on what's happening right now. Like this beautiful day, hanging out with friends."

Emma put down her phone and looked around. "You know, you might be onto something."

Sophia smiled. "Let's try something. Let's put our phones away for a bit and just be here, in the moment."

Reluctantly, her friends agreed. They put their phones in the centre of the blanket and leaned back, looking up at the sky. At first, it felt strange, but soon they found themselves talking and laughing, enjoying each other's company without the constant pull of their devices.

As the afternoon passed, Sophia felt a sense of peace she hadn't felt in a long time. It reminded her of the way she felt when she focused on her homework without distractions. She realized that being present wasn't just a tool for schoolwork; it was a way to truly experience life.

The following week, Sophia's math teacher, Mr. Thompson, announced a surprise quiz. The class groaned, but Sophia took a deep breath and reminded herself to stay in the present moment. She focused on each question, blocking out the stress and worry about her grade. When the quiz was over, she felt confident she had done well.

After school, Sophia's friends gathered at their usual spot. They had started meeting regularly to study together, each of them trying to incorporate the present moment focus into their routines. It was working; their grades were improving, and they felt less stressed.

Sophia decided to share a story her mother had told her, hoping it would inspire her friends even more.

"Years ago," she began, "my mom met an old man named Eli who lived in a small cottage at the edge of town. His garden was full of blooming flowers and vegetables, a place that felt magical. She used to visit him to escape her worries, and one day, she confessed her struggles with school to him."

"He smiled and told her, 'Math and reading are not hard, they're just misunderstood. You're just not living in the present moment.' She didn't understand what he meant, so he explained. 'When you worry about how difficult something will be, or when you think about past failures, you are not giving your full attention to the present moment. The present is where the magic happens.'"

Sophia's friends listened intently, much like she had in the beginning.

"Eli took my mom to his garden and showed her how to plant seeds. 'Each seed is like a moment,' he said. 'If you focus on planting it well, it will grow strong. But if you're distracted, it might not even take root.' He taught her to concentrate on one thing at a time, whether it was solving a math problem or reading a paragraph. By being fully present, she found that the answers became clearer and her understanding deeper."

Alex nodded thoughtfully. "That's a great analogy. It makes sense. If we focus on each moment, we can plant seeds of understanding and grow our knowledge."

Sophia smiled. "Exactly. So, let's keep practising this, not just with our studies, but in everything we do."

As the weeks turned into months, Sophia and her friends continued to support each other in their new approach to life. They became more mindful, not just in school, but in their daily interactions. They found joy in the little things—watching a sunset, enjoying a meal, or simply spending time together without distractions.

One day, Ms. Alvarez asked the class to write an essay about a personal challenge they had overcome. Sophia wrote about her struggle with math and reading and how focusing on the present moment had changed everything for her.

When she got her essay back, she saw a note from Ms. Alvarez: "Excellent job, Sophia! You've discovered a valuable life skill. Keep it up!"

Sophia smiled, feeling proud. She knew that no matter what challenges came her way, she had the power of the present moment to guide her.

Her story didn't just end there. Sophia continued to share her experiences and the lessons she had learned with others, spreading the message of the power of the present moment. She joined the school's peer mentoring program, helping younger students who were struggling with the same issues she had faced.

Through her journey, Sophia discovered that being present wasn't just about improving grades or understanding subjects better; it was about truly living and experiencing life to the fullest. She realized that the world was filled with beauty and opportunities that could easily be missed if she was constantly distracted by worries and devices.

Years later, as she prepared for her high school graduation, Sophia looked back on her journey with gratitude. She had not only overcome her academic challenges but had also built strong, meaningful relationships and developed a deep appreciation for life.

Standing at the podium to deliver her valedictorian speech, she looked out at her classmates and smiled. "I want to share something with you all that changed my life. It's simple, yet powerful: the present moment. When we focus on the now, we can overcome any challenge, find joy in the little things, and truly live our lives to the fullest. Remember, each moment is like a seed. Plant it well, and watch it grow into something beautiful."

The audience erupted in applause, and Sophia felt a deep sense of fulfilment. She knew that as she moved forward into the next chapter of her life, she would carry the lessons of the present moment with her, ready to face any challenge that came her way.

And so, the seeds of the present moment continued to grow, not just in.

Now, I am sure you can understand the answer to the question-

How many times you are present in your timeless present moment?

LAXMI MITTAL

An amazing question from the book Power of Now by Echart Tolle –

Are you a habitual "waiter"?

"How much of your life do you spend waiting?"

What I call "small scale waiting" is waiting in line at the post office, in a traffic jam, at the airport or waiting for someone to arrive, to finish work, and so on." large scale waiting "is waiting for the next vacation, for the better job, for children to grow up, for a significant relationship, for success, to make money, to become important, to become enlightened. it is not uncommon for people to spend their whole lives waiting to start living.

Waiting is a state of mind it means that you want the future; you don't want the present. you don't want what you have got. You want what you haven't got. with every waiting, you unconsciously create inner conflict between your here and now, where you don't want to be and the projected future, where you want to be. This greatly reduces the quality of life by making you lose the present.

By losing your present, by losing your 'Now', you are like an architect who pays no attention to the foundation of a building but spends a lot of time working on superstructure.

So, you need to honour, acknowledge and fully accept your present reality- where you are, who you are, what you are reading, what you doing right now, -then you fully accept what you have got in the present moment.

So, give up waiting as a state of mind. When you catch yourself slipping into waiting out of it. come into the present moment. if you are present, there is never any need for you to wait for anything. so next time somebody says," Sorry, to keep you waiting,' you can reply, "That's all right, I was not waiting. I was just standing here enjoying myself the quality of your success depends on the quality of consciousness in the present moment — in joy in myself."

By being present in your present moment - 'Now' you are in a state of intense presence, you are free of thought. You are still, yet highly alert. The instant your attention sinks below a certain level, thought rushes in. The mental noise returns; the stillness is lost.

You are back in time otherwise the present moment is timeless.

So, be present in your present moment, to get free from anxiety, fear, stress of your studies or success. The present moment is time-less and painless. Consciousness in the present moment is the only key to giving your best, to do your best.

To be fully present in the 'Now', practice Super Brain yoga, a simple yet extraordinarily powerful exercise.

Super Brain Yoga is an ancient practice that involves a simple yet powerful exercise designed to enhance cognitive function and boost energy levels. It combines physical movement with specific breathing techniques and aims to activate and synchronize brain hemispheres, improve mental clarity, and boost overall brain power.

*Scan the QR Code for Su-
per Brain Yoga*

To perform Super Brain Yoga, follow these steps:

1. Preparation:

- Stand with your feet shoulder-width apart, ideally facing east for maximum benefit as per traditional practice. It is recommended to remove any jewellery before beginning the exercise.

2. Hand Position:

- Hold your right earlobe with your left hand, placing the thumb in front of the lobe and the fingers at the back.

- Cross your right arm over your chest and hold your left earlobe with your right hand using the same hand position, ensuring the thumb is in front.

3. Breathing Technique:

- Inhale deeply through your nose as you squat down slowly, keeping your back straight.

- Hold your breath briefly at the bottom of the squat.

4. Movement:

- Exhale slowly through your nose as you rise back to a standing position.

- Repeat this squatting and breathing cycle 15-21 times, maintaining the hand position and focusing on your breath.

5. Completion:

- Release your hands and stand still for a few moments to feel the effects of the exercise.

Super Brain Yoga is a simple yet effective practice that can be incorporated into your daily routine to support mental clarity and overall brain health.

Super Brain Yoga offers a multitude of benefits, making it a valuable addition to your daily routine. Here are some of the key advantages:

1. Enhances Cognitive Function: Through regular practice, Super Brain Yoga is believed to enhance memory, concentration, and mental clarity by synchronizing the brain's hemispheres. This synchronization can lead to improved cognitive function.

2. Reduces Stress and Anxiety: The combination of rhythmic breathing and physical movement involved in Super Brain Yoga promotes relaxation and helps reduce stress levels, providing a calming effect on the mind and body.

3. Increases Energy Levels: Super Brain Yoga stimulates the flow of energy in the body, thereby enhancing overall vitality and reducing fatigue. This increase in energy levels can lead to improved productivity and an overall sense of well-being.

4. Improves Emotional Balance: By activating specific acupuncture points on the earlobes, Super Brain Yoga assists in regulating emotional stability and balance, contributing to improved overall emotional well-being.

5. Promotes Better Learning: Super Brain Yoga is especially beneficial for students and individuals engaged in mentally demanding tasks, as it helps improve focus and information retention. Incorporating this practice into your routine may lead to enhanced learning abilities and academic performance.

Incorporating Super Brain Yoga into your daily routine offers a natural and holistic approach to boosting brain health and overall well-being. Just 59 seconds a day can make a significant difference in your cognitive function, emotional balance, and energy levels.In order to alleviate the anxiety, fear, and stress related to your studies or pursuit of success, it's essential to fully engage in your present moment. By being fully present, you can transcend time and discomfort. Maintaining consciousness in the present moment is the key to unlocking your best performance.

5 Key Takeaways: Power of the Present Moment

1. Present Moment Awareness: Focus on the present to avoid being controlled by past regrets or future anxieties.

2. Mental Exercise: Simple exercises like deep breathing can reveal how often the mind drifts from the present.

3. Practical Example: Sophia's story illustrates how focusing on the present moment can improve understanding and performance in daily tasks.

4. Eckhart Tolle's Insight: Recognize and reduce habitual waiting to fully live in the present.

5. Super Brain Yoga: Practice Super Brain Yoga to enhance cognitive function, reduce stress, and improve emotional balance through physical and breathing techniques.

CHAPTER 7

EMBRACE CHALLENGES WITH CONFIDENCE

On the day of our Independence, I always look forward to watching kites soaring higher and higher in the vast blue sky. The colourful kites against the backdrop of the open sky symbolise boundless happiness, unity, and freedom. It's a sight that fills my heart with joy. Additionally, I love the sight of balloons floating higher and higher and witnessing flocks of birds taking flight - it's a truly uplifting experience.

The beauty of these scenes always fills me with an intense desire to soar higher and higher. One evening, this feeling prompted a question: How can I experience flying in the sky? The answer was fairly simple - I needed to book a flight ticket. Following this realisation, my elder brother, Mr. Brij Mohan, graciously arranged for my first flight experience and the elation I felt lingered for many days. Naturally, this only fuelled my desire for more airborne adventures.

During this period, I had the privilege of attending a session led by my spiritual mentor, Ms. R Lakshmi Dhevi. She posed a thought-provoking question - who can soar high? What prevents humans from taking flight? She pointed out that one of the essential characteristics for something to take flight is lightness. Emotionally, we tend to carry a heavy burden, filled with deep-seated anger, jealousy, and frustration, which act as barriers to achieving flight in every aspect of our lives. This revelation was truly eye-opening for me.

Seeking a solution to unburden ourselves from this emotional baggage, I asked my mentor for advice. She provided a simple yet powerful solution - to spend 5 minutes daily practising forgiveness. By doing so, we can embrace challenges with confidence and become emotionally lighter, allowing us to soar to greater heights in all aspects of our lives.

Mathematics can be a challenging subject for many teenagers because of its intricate, abstract concepts and the precise nature of its equations. Students often feel intimidated by the complexity of the subject. However, they need to embrace these challenges as they are crucial for both academic success and personal growth. By approaching the learning process with the principles of forgiveness and the Golden Rule, students can make this journey more manageable and rewarding. This approach not only enhances the learning experience but also contributes to personal development in numerous ways.

Understanding the Challenge

Mathematics is a subject that follows a logical progression, where mastery of foundational concepts is essential for understanding more advanced ideas. This sequential nature means that gaps in comprehension can impede learning and contribute to a fear of failure. Adolescents frequently experience significant academic pressure, particularly in the realm of mathematics, which can result in heightened anxiety and a disheartened approach to the subject.

Embracing Forgiveness

Self-Forgiveness

Understanding the power of self-forgiveness is crucial in helping students overcome the fear of failure in mathematics. Mistakes are an inevitable part of the learning process, and acknowledging this fact can significantly reduce the pressure that students experience. When students learn to forgive themselves for making errors, they cultivate a positive mindset that encourages resilience and growth.

Self-forgiveness in math entails recognizing that every individual, regardless of their proficiency in mathematics, is prone to making mistakes. Each mistake presents an opportunity for learning and improvement. By shifting the focus from the pursuit of perfection to the journey of progress, students can approach challenges with a healthier and more constructive attitude. This shift in perspective not only reduces the fear of failure but also fosters a more positive and resilient approach to learning mathematics.

Forgiving Others

In the context of mathematics education, it is often beneficial to engage in group study sessions and collaborative projects. These settings provide opportunities for students to work together, share ideas, and learn from each other. It is important to cultivate an environment of understanding and forgiveness within these groups. When a peer makes a mistake, it should be seen as a chance for everyone to learn and grow, rather than a cause for frustration. This approach not only strengthens the bond within the group but also fosters a supportive learning atmosphere where every member feels appreciated and respected for their contributions.

The Golden Rule of Mathematics

The Golden Rule advises treating others as you would like to be treated, which is a timeless and universal principle. When this principle is embraced in the learning environment, it fosters a nurturing and motivating atmosphere that encourages respect, empathy, and cooperation among students and educators.

Mutual Respect and Encouragement

In any classroom or study group setting, it is crucial to prioritise mutual respect. When students show kindness and patience towards one another, they actively contribute to building a positive and supportive learning environment. This respect encompasses recognising and appreciating that every individual learns at their own pace and possesses their own set of strengths and weaknesses. A culture of encouragement can be especially impactful; when students support and uplift one another, they establish a close-knit community of learners who are unafraid to take on challenging academic tasks.

Constructive Criticism

Effective feedback is an essential component of the learning process in mathematics. Feedback must be delivered constructively. Adhering to the Golden Rule, feedback should be given in a way that the giver would appreciate receiving it—offered positively and constructively. Instead of merely pointing out errors, constructive criticism centres on providing guidance for improvement, and offering specific and actionable advice. This approach fosters an environment where students can learn from their mistakes without feeling demoralised, ultimately enhancing their overall learning experience.

Mindful Techniques for Learning Mathematics

Incorporating mindfulness practices into the process of learning mathematics has the potential to amplify the positive effects of forgiveness and the Golden Rule. Mindfulness entails being completely attentive and involved in the present moment, a state of mind that can assist students in coping with anxiety and enhancing their ability to concentrate. This approach has the potential to profoundly impact the learning experience, helping students develop a more holistic understanding of mathematics while also cultivating important life skills.

Mindful Breathing

Before beginning a math session, it can be beneficial for students to engage in some mindfulness techniques such as deep, mindful breathing. Mindful breathing allows students to centre themselves, reduce stress, and prepare their minds for focused work. This simple yet powerful technique is especially useful before tests or when approaching particularly challenging math problems. By taking a few moments to focus on their breath, students can create a sense of calm and mental clarity, ultimately improving their ability to tackle complex mathematical concepts.

Staying Present

When working on mathematics, maintaining a high level of concentration is crucial. Mindfulness practices can help students develop the ability to stay present and focused, preventing them from feeling overwhelmed by the complexity of the problems. By approaching problems with a mindful mindset, students can learn to break them down into smaller, more manageable steps. This approach allows them to concentrate on one aspect at a time, effectively reducing anxiety and enhancing their problem-solving skills.

Reflective Practice

After finishing a set of math problems, students need to pause and engage in reflective practice. This involves carefully analysing the strategies they used, identifying those that were effective and those that weren't, and considering how they can enhance their approach in the future. By engaging in this reflective process, students not only solidify their understanding of the material but also cultivate a growth mindset. This mindset encourages them to view challenges as chances for growth and development rather than as daunting barriers.

Integrating Forgiveness and the Golden Rule with Mindfulness

Integrating forgiveness, the Golden Rule and mindfulness create a comprehensive and enriching approach to teaching and learning mathematics. By implementing these principles, educators can cultivate an environment where students feel safe to make mistakes, collaborate effectively, and develop a growth mindset.

1. ***Creating a Safe Learning Environment:*** Teachers play a key role in establishing a classroom culture where making mistakes is not only accepted but encouraged as an essential part of the learning process. By fostering an atmosphere of forgiveness and understanding, students learn to embrace their fallibility and develop resilience. This involves practising self-forgiveness and forgiving others, promoting empathetic and respectful interactions, and providing constructive feedback that focuses on growth and improvement rather than judgment.

2. ***Promoting Collaboration:*** Encouraging collaborative learning experiences can be a powerful way to integrate the Golden Rule into the mathematics classroom. By engaging in group work and peer teaching, students learn to treat others as they would like to be treated, creating an environment of mutual respect and support. Peer teaching not only reinforces the understanding of mathematical concepts but also nurtures leadership skills and empathy among students.

3. ***Incorporating Mindfulness Practices:*** Introducing mindfulness exercises into the curriculum can help students develop metacognitive awareness and emotional regulation skills. By engaging in regular mindfulness activities such as mindful breathing, reflective journaling, and guided visualisation, students can learn to manage stress and enhance their focus and attention. Mindfulness practices can also foster a sense of curiosity and open-mindedness, encouraging students to approach mathematical challenges with a calm and centred mindset.

4. ***Encouraging a Growth Mindset:*** Emphasizing the idea that intelligence and mathematical ability are not fixed traits but skills that can be developed through effort and perseverance is essential for nurturing a growth mindset. By integrating forgiveness, respect, and mindfulness practices, educators can help students cultivate a positive outlook on learning, where challenges are seen as opportunities for growth rather than obstacles. This approach encourages students to persist in the face of difficulties, ultimately leading to increased motivation and academic resilience.

Practical Tips for Students

1. *Set Realistic Goals:* When setting goals for your math studies, it's important to break them down into manageable steps. By setting realistic goals, you can track your progress and celebrate small victories along the way, which will keep you motivated and focused.

2. *Practice Regularly:* Consistency is key to mastering mathematics. Regular practice not only helps reinforce concepts but also improves problem-solving skills. Make it a habit to incorporate math practice into your daily routine to see the best results.

3. *Seek Help When Needed:* It's perfectly okay to ask for help when you're struggling with a math concept. Whether it's reaching out to your teacher, seeking assistance from peers, or getting support from tutors, understanding that seeking help is part of the learning process and it's essential for self-forgiveness and respecting your learning journey.

4. *Use Positive Self-Talk:* Instead of dwelling on negative thoughts about your math abilities, replace them with positive affirmations. Remind yourself that making mistakes is a normal part of the learning process and that you can improve with effort and practice.

5. *Engage in Group Studies:* Collaborating with peers in a respectful and supportive manner can be extremely beneficial. Participating in group studies allows you to share knowledge, encourage each other, and practice the Golden Rule by treating others the way you would like to be treated. Working together with peers can provide different perspectives and approaches to problem-solving, enriching your learning experience.

Conclusion

Embracing challenges in learning mathematics goes beyond just using cognitive effort. It also involves cultivating the right mindset and environment. By practising forgiveness - letting go of past mistakes and not being too hard on oneself, applying the Golden Rule - treating others as you would like to be treated, and incorporating mindfulness techniques - such as deep breathing and focusing on the present moment, teenagers can transform their approach to mathematics. This holistic strategy not only enhances their mathematical skills but also fosters personal growth, resilience, and a positive attitude towards lifelong learning.

5 Key Takeaways: Embrace Challenges with Confidence

1. Symbol of Freedom: Kites, balloons, and birds symbolize happiness, unity, and freedom, inspiring a desire to soar higher.

2. First Flight: Booking a flight ticket with the help of my brother ignited a passion for airborne adventures.

3. Spiritual Insight: My mentor taught that emotional lightness, achieved through forgiveness, is essential for personal growth.

4. Daily Forgiveness: Practicing five minutes of forgiveness daily can help overcome emotional burdens and elevate life.

5. Mathematics and Mindfulness: Combining forgiveness, the Golden Rule, and mindfulness can transform the learning experience in challenging subjects like mathematics.

Chapter 8

DEVELOP RESILIENCE AND UNLOCK THE SUPERPOWER

To grow resilient, it's important to tap into the incredible strength that resides within each of us. This superpower, you may wonder, is gratitude. By cherishing every aspect of our lives, big and small, we activate a kind of magic lens. This lens allows us to see the beauty and positivity in life, even during tough times. It's like wearing a pair of special glasses that enable us to see the silver lining in every situation, regardless of the challenges we face.

Let us move to the life of blessed Sarah. She was a typical teenager. She had all the comforts a teenager could ask for A loving family, a cosy home, and all the latest gadgets. Yet, like many teenagers, she often found herself complaining about minor inconveniences.

She wished she had a better phone, she disliked her school, and she frequently argued with her parents over trivial matters.

One day, Sarah's mother suggested that they spend a Saturday volunteering at the local homeless shelter. Reluctantly, Sarah agreed, thinking it would be a boring and uncomfortable experience. She couldn't imagine how spending a day with homeless people could have any impact on her life.

When they arrived at the shelter, Sarah was immediately struck by the stark difference between her life and the lives of the people there. She met families who had lost their homes due to unforeseen circumstances, veterans who were struggling to reintegrate into society, and children who were just like her, but without the stability and security she took for granted.

As Sarah served food and chatted with the shelter's residents, she heard stories that deeply moved her. There was Mr Thompson, a former engineer who had lost his job and home after a series of unfortunate events. Despite his situation, he remained hopeful and grateful for the small things in life, like the kindness of strangers and the warmth of a meal.

Sarah also met a young girl named Lily, who was her age. Lily had been living in the shelter with her mother for several months after escaping an abusive household. Despite her hardships, Lily was cheerful and full of dreams for the future. She was grateful for the shelter and the opportunity to go to school every day, something Sarah had always taken for granted.

Throughout the day, Sarah's perspective began to shift. She realized how much she had overlooked the blessings in her own life. The complaints that once seemed so significant now felt trivial in comparison to the challenges faced by the people at the shelter.

On the ride home, Sarah was quiet, reflecting on what she had experienced. That evening, she thanked her parents for taking her to the shelter and for everything they had done for her. She felt a newfound appreciation for her life and the people in it.

The experience stayed with Sarah, and she decided to continue volunteering at the shelter. Each time she went, she learned more about the residents and their stories. This not only deepened her sense of gratitude but also inspired her to help others and make a difference in her community.

Sarah's story is a powerful lesson in gratitude. It shows that sometimes, stepping out of our comfort zone and seeing the world from a different perspective can profoundly impact our appreciation for what we have. The moral of the story is that gratitude isn't just about saying "thank you" but about recognising and valuing the blessings in our lives, no matter how small they may seem.

Remembering to be grateful can completely shift our mindset. When we consciously practice gratitude, we direct our focus to the things we have and the positive qualities we possess, rather than dwelling on what we lack. This simple shift can lead to a more positive outlook on life. Here are some ways that practising gratitude can benefit us:

1. Improved Well-being: By acknowledging and appreciating the things we have, we can experience increased happiness, positivity, and decreased stress.

2. Stronger Relationships: Gratitude helps in nurturing and building stronger connections with others, making us more resilient when facing challenges.

3. Appreciating Life's Joys: It reminds us to cherish the simple pleasures in life, such as a beautiful sunset, a kind word from a friend, or a warm embrace.

Now, let's explore a practical approach to incorporating gratitude into our lives:

Practising gratitude is accessible to everyone and can be seamlessly integrated into our daily routines. One effective method is to maintain a gratitude journal. Each evening, take a moment to reflect on your day, identify moments or things that you are grateful for, and jot them down. This simple act of acknowledgement can have a profound impact on our mindset.

For instance:

- I am grateful for the good health that allows me to enjoy life. Thank you! Thank you! Thank you!

- I am grateful for the unwavering support of my family. Thank you! Thank you! Thank you!

- I am thankful for the opportunity to learn and grow at my school. Thank you! Thank you! Thank you!

- I am appreciative of the books and the authors who have enriched my life with knowledge and stories. Thank you! Thank you! Thank you!

By focusing on these positive aspects, we train our minds to perceive the world in a more optimistic light. Expressing our gratitude not only benefits us but also spreads kindness and positivity to those around us, whether it's an acknowledgement of a teacher's guidance or a friend's support.

So, congratulations! By embracing the practice of gratitude, you have unlocked a potent superpower. Incorporating gratitude into your daily life can significantly brighten your days, imbue them with joy, and lead to a more fulfilling existence. So, put on those gratitude glasses and watch the world around you sparkle with positivity and joy!

5 Key Takeaways: Develop Resilience and Unlock the Superpower

1. Gratitude Superpower: Embracing gratitude helps us see the beauty and positivity in life, even during tough times.

2. Perspective Shift: Volunteering at a homeless shelter transformed Sarah's outlook, highlighting the blessings in her life.

3. Impactful Stories: Hearing stories from shelter residents deepened Sarah's appreciation and inspired her to help others.

4. Ongoing Practice: Sarah continued volunteering, reinforcing her gratitude and commitment to making a difference.

5. Daily Gratitude: Maintaining a gratitude journal can improve well-being, strengthen relationships, and enhance appreciation for life's joys.

Chapter 9

BUILDING A GROWTH MINDSET IN MATHEMATICS

"It's your Attitude, not your Aptitude that will determine your Altitude"

– Zig Ziglar

In mathematics, there exists a concept known as the Golden Rule for learning. This principle emphasises the importance of cultivating a growth mindset in mathematical endeavours. The crux of this rule lies in the notion that one's abilities and intelligence are not fixed, but rather malleable and can be enhanced through unwavering dedication, perseverance, and continuous learning.

To put it simply, having a growth mindset entails believing that one can improve their skills through deliberate effort and consistent practice. With this mindset, individuals embrace the idea that they can conquer any challenge and achieve mastery of various mathematical concepts. This outlook is particularly advantageous in the context of learning mathematics as it fosters a positive approach towards difficulties and errors, recognising them as integral components of the learning process.

Why does a Growth Mindset matter in Math?

Understanding the importance of having a growth mindset in the context of mathematics is crucial. Many individuals find math challenging and daunting, often leading to feelings of frustration and being stuck when facing difficult concepts. However, it's essential to recognise that mathematical proficiency is not an inborn talent but rather a skill that can be developed over time. Even renowned mathematicians had to invest time, make errors, and continuously learn to excel in their field.

Adopting a growth mindset enables individuals to perceive mistakes as valuable opportunities for learning and development. Each mathematical problem encountered serves as an opportunity to enhance one's skills, contributing to increased intelligence and capability in mathematics. Coined by psychologist Carol Dweck, the concept of a growth mindset revolves around the belief that dedication and hard work can lead to the development of abilities and intelligence.

For teenagers, especially, embracing a growth mindset is vital in overcoming the fear of failure and embracing the learning journey in mathematics. This mindset shift allows them to approach mathematical challenges with resilience and a willingness to learn, ultimately fostering a more positive and productive relationship with the subject.

Fixed Mindset Vs Growth Mindset

Understanding the distinction between a fixed mindset and a growth mindset is crucial before delving into strategies for fostering a growth mindset. Dr Carol S. Dweck has provided an insightful explanation of these concepts.

1. *Fixed Mindset:* Individuals with a fixed mindset believe that their intelligence and abilities are innate and cannot be changed. They tend to shy away from challenges, give up quickly when faced with obstacles, and consider the effort to be in vain if they don't achieve immediate success.

2. *Growth Mindset:* On the other hand, individuals with a growth mindset believe that their intelligence and abilities can be developed through dedicated effort, persistence, and learning from failures. Those with a growth mindset willingly take on challenges, endure difficulties, and perceive the effort as a means to mastery.

How to Apply the Golden Rule in Math Learning

Now that you understand the importance of a growth mindset, let's talk about how you can apply this golden rule to your math learning. Here are five key strategies:

1. Embrace Challenges

Don't shy away from difficult problems. Challenges are what make your brain stronger. When you face a tough problem, approach it with the belief that you can figure it out with effort and persistence. Remember, each challenge you tackle helps you grow much stronger.

2. Learn from Mistakes and reduce Math Anxiety

Mistakes are not failures; they are valuable learning opportunities. When you make a mistake, take the time to understand what went wrong and how you can fix it. This process of reflection and correction is essential for learning and improvement. By seeing mistakes as part of the learning process, you can reduce their fear of failure and anxiety around math.

3. Stay Persistent and improve problem-solving skills

Persistence is key to mastering any new skill, including math. Keep working at it, even when it feels difficult or frustrating. Remember that every bit of effort counts and gets you closer to your goals. The more you practice, the better you'll become. A willingness to tackle challenging problems and learn from mistakes enhances critical thinking and problem-solving skills.

4. Seek Feedback

Don't be afraid to ask for help or feedback. Whether it's from your teachers, friends, or online resources, getting different perspectives can help you understand a concept better. Feedback is a valuable tool for improvement.

5. Celebrate Effort

Recognise and celebrate your hard work and progress, not just the result. It's important to appreciate the effort you're putting in, even if you haven't mastered a concept yet. Every bit of effort brings you closer to success.

Real-Life Stories

Consider the incredible power of a growth mindset by taking a look at real-life examples. Let's delve into some inspiring stories where each setback was viewed as a stepping stone towards success.

Story 1: Albert Einstein

Albert Einstein's life is a testament to the power of a growth mindset. Despite facing numerous challenges as a young student, he demonstrated an unwavering determination to understand the world around him. Einstein's struggle with speech fluency until the age of nine led his teachers to believe he was intellectually disabled, and he encountered difficulties in school, particularly with rote learning. Additionally, he initially failed the entrance exam to the Swiss Federal Polytechnic in Zurich due to linguistic problems.

However, Einstein did not allow these setbacks to define his potential. Instead, he focused on his interests in mathematics and physics, driven by a deep passion to uncover the mysteries of the universe. Through perseverance and dedication, he ultimately developed the groundbreaking theory of relativity, which revolutionised our understanding of physics.

Einstein's story serves as a powerful reminder that initial struggles do not determine one's potential for success. By embracing challenges and persisting through difficulties, students can achieve remarkable accomplishments.

Story 2: Mary Jackson (American Mathematician and aerospace engineer)

Mary Jackson, a pioneering African-American woman, overcame significant barriers to become one of the first female engineers at

NASA. Growing up in a segregated school system, Mary encountered numerous obstacles in her pursuit of education. Despite these challenges, she demonstrated exceptional determination and excelled in mathematics and science.

Upon joining NASA, Mary aspired to become an engineer, but she faced initial rejection due to racial discrimination. Undeterred, she undertook night classes in mathematics and physics while simultaneously fighting for admission to an all-white high school to attend additional courses. Her resilience and perseverance ultimately led to her achieving her goal of becoming an aerospace engineer and making substantial contributions to the space program.

Mary Jackson's inspirational journey underscores the significance of resilience, continuous learning, and the transformative power of viewing challenges as opportunities for personal and professional growth. Her story serves as a powerful example, motivating individuals to confront adversity with determination and tenacity.

Story 3: Maryam Mirzakhani

In the realm of Mathematics, take the story of Maryam Mirzakhani into account. She made history as the first woman to be awarded the prestigious Fields Medal. Throughout her journey, she encountered numerous obstacles and experienced setbacks. However, her unwavering commitment to a growth mindset enabled her to overcome these challenges and ultimately attain remarkable success.

Early Life and Challenges

Born in Tehran, Iran, in 1977, Maryam Mirzakhani showed an early interest in reading and writing. Initially, she had no particular inclination toward mathematics. She did not always excel in the subject during her early school years.

Overcoming Obstacles

Mirzakhani faced numerous obstacles on her path to success. Growing up during the Iran-Iraq War, she experienced significant disruptions in her education. Despite these challenges, she maintained her curiosity and determination. She participated in the Iranian National Math Olympiad, initially failing to make the team but persisting and eventually winning gold medals in consecutive years.

After high school, Mirzakhani attended Sharif University of Technology in Tehran, where she continued to excel. Her perseverance and hard work paid off when she moved to the United States to pursue a PhD at Harvard University. Under the mentorship of Curtis McMullen, a Fields Medallist himself, she flourished, focusing on complex geometric and dynamic systems.

Major Contributions and Legacy

Maryam Mirzakhani's contributions to mathematics are profound and wide-ranging. Her work in understanding the symmetry of curved surfaces, particularly in the context of hyperbolic geometry, moduli spaces, and ergodic theory, has had a significant impact on both pure mathematics and theoretical physics.

Her groundbreaking research earned her the Fields Medal in 2014. In her acceptance speech, she humbly reflected on the importance of persistence and passion in her work. Her achievements have inspired countless young women and men across the world to pursue their interests in mathematics, showcasing the power of a growth mindset.

Conclusion

As you begin your mathematical journey, always keep in mind the Golden Rule of a growth mindset. Embrace the belief in your capacity to learn and develop, maintain a sense of curiosity, and continue challenging yourself. Remember, proficiency in mathematics is not about attaining perfection; it's about progress and finding enjoyment in the learning process. With a growth mindset, you have the power to unleash your complete potential and accomplish remarkable feats. You've got what it takes to succeed!

Developing a growth mindset in mathematics is a transformative process that demands intentional effort and the implementation of various strategies. By actively changing how mistakes are perceived, establishing achievable goals, fostering a positive learning environment, and modelling a growth mindset, individuals can embrace challenges and perceive their abilities as malleable.

This mindset not only enriches the experience of learning mathematics but also equips individuals with the resilience and skills for lifelong success in various aspects of life. It's important to celebrate the efforts you put in as you embark on this exciting journey of learning and personal growth!

5 Key Takeaways: Building a Growth Mindset in Mathematics

1. Attitude Determines Altitude: Your attitude towards learning and challenges shapes your success more than your initial abilities.

2. Growth Mindset Essentials: Believing in the ability to improve through effort and perseverance is crucial in mastering mathematical concepts.

3. Overcoming Challenges: Embracing a growth mindset allows you to view mistakes as opportunities for learning and growth in mathematics.

4. Fixed vs. Growth Mindset: Contrasting fixed and growth mindsets highlights how believing in your ability to learn enhances your approach to challenges.

5. Practical Strategies: Strategies like embracing challenges, learning from mistakes, seeking feedback, and celebrating effort foster a positive and productive learning environment in mathematics.

CHAPTER 10

HABIT CULTIVATION TO EXCEL IN MATHEMATICS

"The character of an individual is the composition of habits.
Sow a Thought, Reap an Action,
Sow an Action, Reap a Habit,
Sow a Habit, Reap a Character,
Sow a Character, Reap a Destiny"

Stephen R. Covey

Habits play a significant role in shaping an individual's life due to their steadfast nature. Consistency not only fosters discipline but also has the power to transform one's life from good to extraordinary. It sharpens our skills and heightens our awareness. Cultivating positive habits is the key to unlocking our full potential and attaining enduring positive results. The development of habits through consistent efforts directed towards our goals creates momentum, leading to increased productivity and efficiency, thus propelling our progress to unprecedented levels. Our habits exert a strong pull, helping to steer us away from distractions that hinder our growth.

As a teenager, it can be quite challenging to juggle the demands of schoolwork, a social life, and personal interests. Many students find themselves struggling with math anxiety, which can be overcome through consistent studying and effective time management. This guide aims to assist you in developing habits that not only enhance your math skills but also establish a fulfilling daily routine that allows for social media and technology use.

To conquer math anxiety and truly thrive, we must work on unlearning certain habits while acquiring new ones, enabling us to grow from within and pave the way for a successful life.

Habit 1 – Waking up early in the Morning

*"We will have eternity to celebrate the victories but only
a few hours before sunset to win them"*

Amy Carmichael

Why Wake Up Early?

Waking up early can have a positive impact on your overall well-being. By setting your alarm clock a bit earlier than usual, you can create a peaceful and productive start to your day. Here are some benefits of waking up early:

1. ***Enhanced Productivity:*** Early mornings offer a quiet and uninterrupted environment, allowing you to concentrate and be more productive in your tasks.

2. ***Improved Mental Well-being:*** Exposure to the morning light can help regulate your circadian rhythm, boost your mood, and reduce feelings of stress and anxiety.

3. ***Extra Time for Personal Growth:*** Waking up early allows you to engage in activities that contribute to your personal development, such as reading, journaling, exercising, or pursuing hobbies.

By making a habit of waking up early, you can unlock these benefits and set a positive tone for your day.

Establishing a Morning Routine

A well-structured morning routine can significantly impact the way you start your day, setting the tone for productivity and achievement. By following a practical timetable, you can establish the habit of waking up early and incorporating essential activities into your morning. Physical exercise is a crucial component of this routine, contributing to overall health and well-being.

5:00 AM - Wake Up

- Rise immediately when the alarm goes off. Placing the alarm across the room will help you avoid hitting the snooze button.

- Drink a glass of lukewarm water to rehydrate your body and kickstart your metabolism.

5:10 AM - Quick Physical Exercise

- Spend 59 seconds doing Super brain yoga to stimulate mental clarity and focus.

- Engage in an 8-10-minute exercise routine, such as stretching, yoga, or a short run, to increase your energy levels and enhance your mood.

- Practice 5-10 minutes of balancing breathing to calm your mind and prepare for the day ahead.

5:30 AM - 6:30 AM – Victory Hour (Reading Math)

- Dedicate 30-45 minutes to understanding and reviewing math concepts or solving problems during your Victory Hour.

- This quiet time, where your mind is in an alpha state, is ideal for accelerated learning and understanding, with superfast retention.

- Utilize this time for challenging math topics since your mind is fresh and receptive.

6:30 AM - Personal Hygiene and Breakfast

- Take a refreshing shower and prepare for the day ahead.

- Enjoy a nutritious breakfast containing proteins and whole grains to provide sustained energy for your brain.

7:00 AM - School Preparation

- Review your schedule and ensure you have all the necessary materials and completed homework for the school day.

Building Consistent Study Habits

Consistency is crucial for conquering math anxiety and honing your skills. To incorporate math study into your daily routine, consider the following steps:

1. *Daily Review:* Allocate a minimum of 30 minutes every day to work on math. If needed, split this time into two 15-minute sessions to accommodate your schedule.

2. *Set Specific Goals:* Define your daily or weekly math objectives, such as mastering a particular type of problem or concept.

3. *Practice Problems:* Dedicate time to solving a few math problems each day. You can initiate this practice with simpler problems and gradually progress to more challenging ones to enhance your skills further.

Habit 2 – Plan your Day in Advance

Planning your day can greatly enhance your productivity and reduce stress. Here are three practical tips for students to effectively plan their day:

1. Use a Planner or Digital Calendar

To effectively manage your time and stay organized, consider using a planner or a digital calendar. These tools can help you visualize your day, prioritize tasks, and keep track of important deadlines and commitments. Here's how you can make the most of a planner or digital calendar:

1. Evening Planning: Dedicate 10-15 minutes each evening to plan out your next day. Take this time to review your upcoming assignments, tests, extracurricular activities, and any other commitments you may have. This will help you start the day with a clear understanding of what needs to be accomplished.

2. Block Scheduling: Allocate specific time blocks for each activity in your day. This can include time for your classes, study sessions, breaks, meals, and relaxation. By scheduling your day in blocks, you can ensure that you have dedicated time for all of your responsibilities while also allowing for necessary breaks and downtime.

3. Set Priorities: Identify the top three tasks or goals you need to accomplish each day. By focusing on your highest priorities first, you can ensure that you are making progress on the most important tasks, even if unexpected distractions arise later in the day.

4. Digital Tools: Take advantage of digital tools such as Google Calendar, Microsoft Outlook, or specialized student planners like myHomework or Trello. These apps can offer additional features to help you stay organized, set reminders, and easily access your schedule from your devices.

By implementing these strategies, you can effectively manage your time, stay organized, and reduce the stress of juggling multiple commitments as a student.

2. Create a To-Do List with Time Estimates

Keeping a to-do list can be a valuable tool for managing your daily activities and minimizing feelings of overwhelm. By breaking down your day into manageable tasks, you can ensure that you remain focused and on track.

Here's how to effectively utilize a to-do list:

1. Daily To-Do List: Start by listing all the tasks you need to complete for the day. This can include homework, study sessions, work-related tasks, personal activities, and any other responsibilities you need to address.

2. Time Estimates: Once you have listed your tasks, assign a time estimate to each one. This will help you manage your time more effectively and ensure that you allocate sufficient time for each activity.

3. Prioritize Tasks: Arrange your tasks in order of importance or deadline. Tackling high-priority or more challenging tasks when

your energy levels are at their peak can help you make the most of your productive hours.

4. Review and Adjust: At the end of the day, take a moment to review your to-do list. Note down what you have accomplished, and carry over any unfinished tasks to the next day's list. This step allows you to reflect on your productivity and make necessary adjustments for the following day.

By following these steps, you can make the most out of your to-do list and enhance your productivity.

3. Incorporate Buffer Time and Breaks

Don't forget to incorporate buffer time and scheduled breaks into your daily routine to ensure a smooth transition between tasks and to prevent burnout. Taking short breaks (5-10 minutes) between activities or classes allows for any potential overruns or unexpected events. Additionally, it's important to schedule regular breaks during study sessions to rest and recharge.

Habit 3 – Follow the Evening Routine

Here's a detailed workable evening routine that balances enjoyment time, tuition time, self-study, and relaxation:

4:00 PM - Return Home and Relax

- Activity: Unwind from the school day.

- Details: When you return home, take 15-30 minutes to relax. Have a healthy snack to refresh yourself, engage in light conversation with your family, or take a short walk to clear your mind and transition into your evening routine.

4:30 PM - Enjoyment Time

- Activity: Engage in a fun activity.

- Details: Allocate about 30 minutes for an activity you enjoy, such as playing a game, watching a short episode of your favourite show, or catching up on social media. Use a timer to ensure you don't exceed this time and maintain a balance with your other activities.

5:00 PM - Tuition Time

- Activity: Attend tuition classes or receive extra coaching.

- Details: Dedicate 1.5 to 2 hours to focus on subjects that require additional support. Stay attentive during the session, take thorough notes, and actively participate to make the most of this time.

7:00 PM - Short Break

- Activity: Take a break to refresh.

- Details: Spend 15-30 minutes refreshing yourself, having a light dinner, or engaging in casual conversation. It's essential to avoid heavy meals that can lead to drowsiness and affect your evening study sessions.

7:30 PM - Self-Study Session 1

- Activity: Study challenging subjects or topics.

- Details: Allocate 1 hour for studying the subjects you find most challenging or those with upcoming tests. Divide the study material into smaller sections to make the session more manageable and effective.

8:30 PM - Short Break

- Activity: Relax and rejuvenate.

- Details: Take a 15-minute break to stretch, grab a light snack for energy, or briefly engage with social media to unwind. This break will help you recharge before the next study session.

8:45 PM - Self-Study Session 2

- Activity: Focus on easier subjects or homework.

- Details: Spend an additional 1 hour on subjects that come easier to you or complete any pending homework. Use this time to review the day's notes, work on assignments, and reinforce your learning.

9:45 PM - Relaxation and Personal Time

- Activity: Engage in a relaxing activity.

- Details: Dedicate 30 minutes to 1 hour to something that helps you unwind, such as reading a book, listening to music, or enjoying a hobby that brings you joy and relaxation.

10:15 PM - Review and Plan

- Activity: Review the day's studies and plan for tomorrow.

- Details: Spend 15 minutes reviewing what you studied during the day. Take notes of key points and plan the topics to cover the next day. This practice reinforces your learning and helps you prepare for the following day's study sessions.

10:30 PM - Night Routine

- Activity: Wind down for the night.

- Details: Start your night routine by brushing your teeth, washing your face, and engaging in calming activities such as light stretching or any bedtime rituals that help you relax and prepare for a restful night's sleep.

It is important to note that the above-mentioned schedule may be adjusted and personalized according to the student's requirements and preferences.

5 Key Takeaways: Habit Cultivation to Excel in Mathematics

1. Habit Formation: Habits define character and destiny; they start from thoughts and actions, shaping long-term outcomes.

2. Power of Consistency: Consistent habits lead to discipline, sharpening skills, and increasing awareness.

3. Transformative Potential: Positive habits unlock potential, enhancing productivity and efficiency in daily life.

4. Overcoming Challenges: By cultivating new habits and unlearning old ones, teens can conquer challenges like math anxiety.

5. Practical Strategies: Establishing morning and evening routines, planning days, and incorporating buffer times aid in developing effective study habits.

ACTIVITY FOR YOU!

Write your customized Habits and Daily Schedule.

____

____

____

____

____

____

____

____

CHAPTER 11

MATHEMATICAL CREATIVITY AND LEARNING TECHNIQUES

"You can't use up creativity.
The more you use, the more you have.
Creativity is like a muscle that strengthens with re-
peated use."

Mathematics is often perceived as a challenging subject, but with innovative teaching methods, it can become engaging and enjoyable for every student. For Class XI and XII students, who are dealing with advanced concepts, creative learning strategies can make a significant difference in their understanding and appreciation of the subject. Even for each grade student creativity works magically in strengthening the concept. Here are some innovative ideas to enhance the mathematics learning experience for students:

1. Creative Learning Methods

For young students, grasping the concept of fractions can be both time-consuming and challenging. Instead of relying on rote learning, try to incorporate math into your everyday life. Take a look at your mom's kitchen, where you can observe her using measuring spoons and cups, often with measurements printed on them. By paying attention to these tools, you can understand how to compare fractions, relate different fractions to each other, and even convert measurements from tablespoons to cups and vice versa. This practical approach can make learning about fractions much more engaging and understandable.

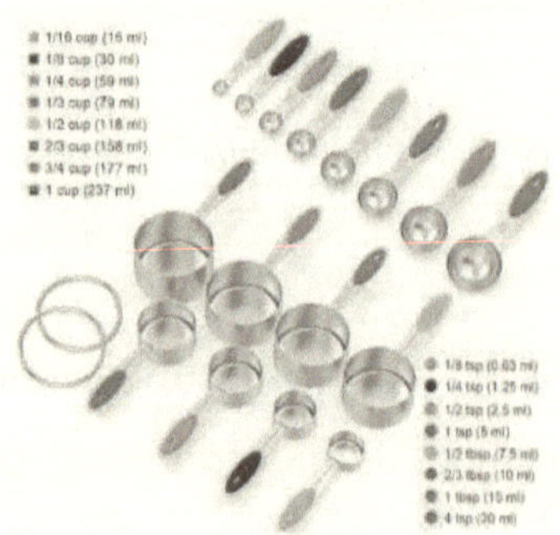

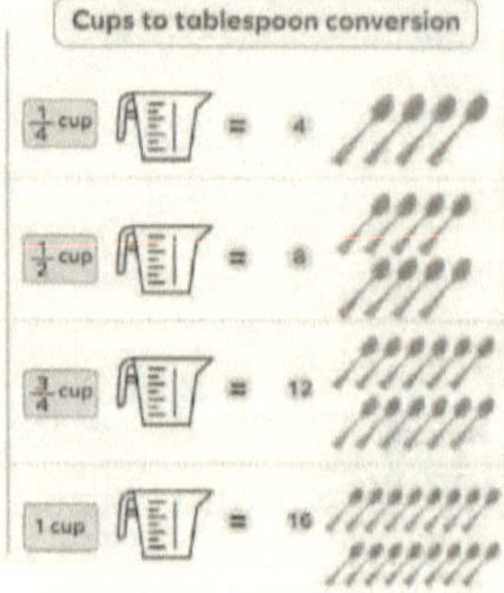

2. Conceptual Understanding

Mathematical pattern generation: Create patterns, stories or real-life scenarios where mathematical concepts are applied. This helps students understand the relevance and application of abstract ideas.

Creating patterns or stories while you solve a word problem related to any topic eases the problem and provides a better understanding and solution to the problem.

Here is a sample for you all with an example of a word problem from the twelfth standard.

Q. Show that the right circular cylinder, open at the top and of given surface area and maximum volume is such that its height is equal to the radius of the base.

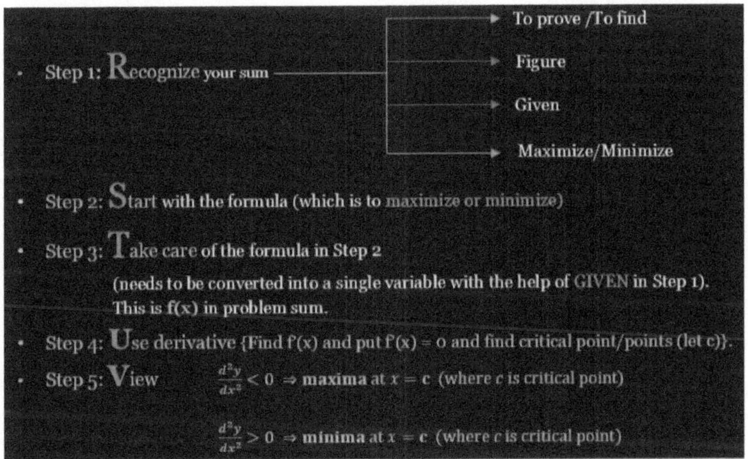

To find the answer, one must first grasp the question. With creative insight, the solution will come effortlessly.

Step 1- Recognise
- figure is right circular cylinder
- Surface area is given
- Volume needs to maximise
- To prove: $h = r$

Step 2 - Start with the formula which needs to maximise i.e.

$$V = \pi r^2 h \quad ---①$$

Step 3- Take care of formula to be converted in single variable using the given dimension in the problem.

$$S = 2\pi r h + \pi r^2$$
$$\Rightarrow h = \frac{S - \pi r^2}{2\pi r} \quad ---②$$

from eq ② in eq ①

$$V = \pi r^2 \left(\frac{S - \pi r^2}{2\pi r}\right) \quad \rightarrow \text{Converted in single Variable}$$

$$V = \pi r^2 \left(\frac{S - \pi r^2}{2\pi r}\right)$$

$$V = \frac{Sr}{2} - \frac{\pi r^3}{2} \quad \Rightarrow \text{Required function}$$

Step 4: Use derivative to find critical point.

$$\frac{dV}{dr} = \frac{S}{2} - \frac{3\pi r^2}{2}$$

Put $\frac{dV}{dr} = 0$

$$\frac{S}{2} = \frac{3\pi r^2}{2}$$

$$S = 3\pi r^2 \quad ---②$$

$$r = \sqrt{\frac{S}{3\pi}}$$

Step-5 View second derivative

$$\frac{d^2V}{dr^2} = -3\pi r$$

$$\left.\frac{d^2V}{dr^2}\right|_{r=\sqrt{\frac{S}{3\pi}}} = -3\pi\sqrt{\frac{S}{3\pi}} < 0$$

$$\Rightarrow V \text{ is maximum.}$$

from eq. ③ in eq ②

$$h = \frac{3\pi r^2 - \pi r^2}{2\pi r} = r$$

Hence required height is equal to radius of its base.

Amazing! How easily this question is being solved.observe the procedure carefully. By breaking the question in five parts R,S,T,U,V(discussed above), solution of a difficult AOD problem has become a cake walk.

3. Visualization and Drawing

In my years of teaching, I have noticed that students often struggle to learn and remember the graphs of inverse trigonometric functions. One evening, I had an idea to make it easier for students to learn and recall these graphs by uniquely visualizing them. I suggested relating each graph to something that already exists, such as an alphabet, posture, pattern, or scene. By making these connections, recalling and remembering the graph becomes much simpler.

For example, to recall the graph of sin inverse, I suggested resembling the curve with the Hindi alphabet 'र' within its domain. By linking the curve to the alphabet, students can remember it more effectively. Similarly, I suggested using a Hindi alphabet (फ) to resemble the curve of the cos inverse, and the swimming butterfly pose to remember the graph of the tan inverse. This method has made learning and recalling these graphs more enjoyable for my students, and they have responded well to this approach.

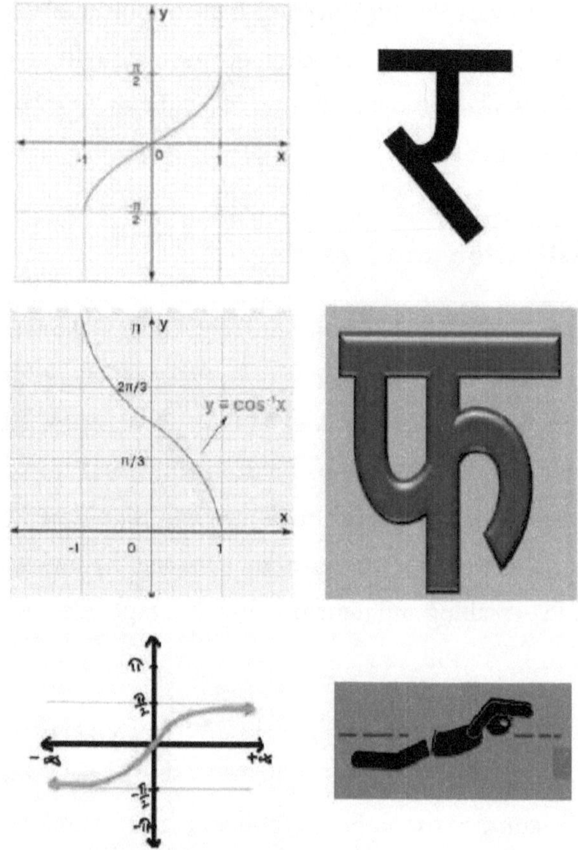

OMG!! How simple is this way or learning/recalling/memorizing the difficult graphs.So,always try to connect graph with the any already existing picture in your mind or surrounding.Then you will enjoy recalling the graph.

4. Technology Integration

Using Educational Software:

• GeoGebra: This versatile tool integrates geometry, algebra, and calculus to allow for dynamic visualization of mathematical concepts and problem-solving.

• Mind Map: Applications such as Canva, XMind, or MindMup can be used to creatively summarize learning on any specific topic using a mind map approach.

• MATLAB and Mathematica: These powerful tools are well-suited for intricate calculations and visualizations, particularly beneficial for gaining insights into calculus and linear algebra.

Online Platforms and Resources:

• Desmos: This online graphing calculator is an excellent resource for exploring functions, plotting graphs, and comprehending transformations.

5. Interactive Learning Techniques

Gamification:

- Math Games and Apps: Utilize apps such as "DragonBox" and "Mathletics" to transform math problems into interactive and enjoyable games, providing an engaging approach to learning.

- Quizzes and Competitions: Participate in Math bees, quizzes, and online competitions to promote a competitive yet enjoyable learning atmosphere, encouraging active engagement and motivation.

Collaborative Learning:

- Peer Teaching: Students are encouraged to engage in peer teaching, where they can explain concepts in their own words to each other, thus deepening their understanding and strengthening their grasp on the material.

6. Incorporating Art and Creativity

Incorporating Mathematics and Art:

- Discovering Geometry in Art: Delve into the world of geometric patterns found in various art forms and architectural designs. Engage in hands-on projects that allow you to produce artwork by applying geometric principles.

- Exploring Fractals and Symmetry: Take an in-depth look at the intricate patterns of fractals and the captivating symmetry present in both nature and art. Embark on creating your very own designs inspired by fractals or crafting symmetrical patterns.

7. Hands-On Activities

When learning mathematics, it's beneficial to incorporate mathematical manipulatives such as physical models. These manipulatives can include 3D shapes, algebra tiles, abacuses, and other physical objects that help students grasp abstract mathematical concepts through hands-on learning.

8. Integration with Other Subjects

Mathematical Poetry: Explore the intersection of mathematics and poetry by challenging yourself to write poems that incorporate mathematical concepts and terminology. Additionally, you can analyse the use of mathematics in literature and historical texts to understand how mathematical themes have been integrated into written works throughout history. Consider assigning readings that include mathematical themes or references to further explore this connection.

8. Mathematical Exploration and Inquiry

Encouraging Inquiry-Based Learning in the Classroom:

Inquiry-based learning involves facilitating an environment where students are encouraged to ask questions and explore multiple ways to solve a problem. This approach fosters a classroom atmosphere where curiosity is highly valued and serves as the foundation of the learning process.

Implementing Effective Questioning Techniques:

Inquiry-based learning can be nurtured by using effective questioning techniques that prompt students to think critically and analytically. By posing open-ended questions, educators can stimulate students' curiosity and provoke thoughtful discussions that lead to deeper understanding.

Utilizing Reflective Mathematical Journals:

Another valuable tool in the Inquiry-Based Learning approach is the use of reflective mathematical journals. These journals provide students with a platform to document their problem-solving processes and reflect on their learning experiences. By encouraging students to write about their mathematical inquiries, educators can help them make connections, identify patterns, and note down new questions and ideas that arise during their learning journey.

9. Utilizing Mathematical History and Culture

Historical Context:

- *Mathematicians' Biographies:* Delve into the biographies of renowned mathematicians, examining their life stories, contributions, and the historical and cultural environments in which they made their discoveries. Gain insight into the challenges they faced and how their work impacted the development of mathematics.

- *Historical Problems:* Engage with historical mathematical problems that have shaped the evolution of mathematical concepts over time. By solving these problems, gain a deeper understanding of the thought processes and mathematical approaches of different eras, and how they have influenced contemporary mathematics.

Cultural Mathematics:

- *Global Perspectives:* Immerse yourself in mathematical concepts from diverse global cultures, such as Vedic mathematics, the Mayan number system, or Chinese mathematical discoveries. Explore the unique approaches and perspectives that different cultures have contributed to the development of mathematics.

- *Cultural Applications:* Investigate the applications of mathematics in architecture, art, and daily life across various cultures. Discover how different societies have used mathematical principles to create iconic architectural structures, develop artistic expressions, and solve practical everyday problems.

One notable mathematical problem from the Ramayana comes from the Sundara Kanda (Book of Beauty), where Hanuman, the devoted follower of Lord Rama, is asked to find Sita, who was abducted by the demon king Ravana and held captive in Lanka.

Hanuman was faced with the challenge of crossing the vast ocean to reach Lanka. He was unsure of his capabilities, but with determination and faith in Lord Rama, he took a mighty leap. As he soared through the sky, he encountered Surasa, a sea demoness who blocked his path.

Surasa told Hanuman that she had been given a divine boon that whoever entered her mouth must come out, as part of her duty to protect the oceans. Hanuman, clever and resourceful, decided to use his wit to outsmart her. He transformed himself into a tiny form and flew directly into Surasa's mouth, then instantly expanded his size, causing Surasa's mouth to stretch infinitely. Hanuman then flew out, fulfilling her divine boon.

This story, while not explicitly a mathematical problem, demonstrates the application of logic and creative problem-solving. It illustrates how Hanuman used his intelligence to navigate a seemingly impossible situation, showcasing the importance of thinking critically and approaching challenges with ingenuity.

This tale from the Ramayana can inspire students to approach mathematical problems with a similar mindset—thinking outside the box, leveraging their knowledge, and using creative strategies to find solutions.

Learning Mathematics to the students requires creativity and innovation to make the subject engaging and relevant. By integrating real-world applications, technology, interactive learning techniques, art, and interdisciplinary approaches, each student can have a deeper understanding and appreciation of mathematics. Encouraging oneself to explore, question, and apply mathematical concepts in diverse ways will not only enhance their learning experience but also prepare them for future academic and professional challenges.

Incorporating these creative ideas into the learning can transform mathematics from a challenging subject into an exciting and rewarding journey of discovery and problem-solving. By nurturing a positive and dynamic learning environment, each student can inspire oneself to develop a lifelong love for mathematics and its myriad applications in the world around them.

5 Key Takeaways: Mathematical Creativity and Learning Techniques

1. Unlimited Creativity: Creativity in learning mathematics is limitless; the more it's used, the more it grows.

2. Enhanced Engagement: Creative methods like integrating math into daily life and storytelling enhance student interest and understanding.

3. Visualization Tools: Using visual aids and analogies, such as relating graphs to familiar shapes, simplifies complex concepts like trigonometric functions.

4. Technology as Enabler: Educational tools like GeoGebra and online platforms like Desmos gamify learning, making math interactive and enjoyable.

5. Interdisciplinary Approach: Integrating art, culture, and historical contexts into math education fosters deeper appreciation and application of mathematical concepts.

CHAPTER 12

NURTURE LOVE FOR MATHEMATICS

"Do the things that you love and bring you joy. If you don't know what brings you joy, ask the question. "What is my joy?" And, as you find it and commit yourself to it, to joy, the law of attraction will pour on the bundle of joyful things, people, circumstances, events and opportunities into your life, all because you are radiating joy."

Rhonda Byrne

Use Affirmations to Develop Love for Mathematics

Affirmations play a crucial role in shaping students' attitudes and beliefs about themselves and their abilities. These positive statements have the power to counteract negative thoughts and self-doubt, ultimately nurturing a more optimistic and constructive mindset towards the learning process. When it comes to the subject of mathematics, affirmations can be particularly transformative for students. By using affirmations, students can develop a genuine passion for mathematics, redefining their academic journey and leading to enhanced performance and a deeper sense of enjoyment in the subject.

What are Affirmations?

Affirmations are simple, positive statements that are repeated regularly to instil belief and confidence in one's abilities. They work by rewiring the brain, helping to replace negative thought patterns with positive ones. When used consistently, affirmations can significantly influence one's mindset and behaviour.

How do Affirmations Work?

1. Positive Reinforcement:

Repeating affirmations reinforces positive beliefs. For example, saying "I am good at math" helps students internalize this belief, leading to increased confidence.

2. Mindset Shift:

Affirmations can shift a student's mindset from fixed to growth-oriented. This change encourages the belief that abilities can be developed through dedication and hard work.

3. Reducing Anxiety:

Positive statements can help reduce math anxiety by replacing fear and worry with calm and confidence. This anxiety reduction can lead to better focus and performance.

Benefits of Using Affirmations for Math

1. Increased Confidence:

Students who use affirmations regularly develop greater confidence in their math abilities, which can lead to improved performance and a more positive attitude towards the subject.

2. Enhanced Motivation:

Affirmations can increase a student's motivation to engage with math, leading to more consistent practice and study.

3. Improved Academic Performance:

As confidence and motivation improve, so does academic performance. Students become more willing to tackle challenging problems and persist through difficulties.

4. Stress Reduction:

Positive affirmations help reduce stress and anxiety, creating a more relaxed and conducive learning environment.

5. Growth Mindset Development:

Affirmations support the development of a growth mindset, where students believe their abilities can improve with effort and persistence.

How to write Effective Affirmations?

Writing effective affirmations involves a few key principles:

1. Use Present Tense:

Affirmations should be written in the present tense as if the desired outcome is already happening. For example, "I am improving in math every day."

2. Be Positive:

Focus on what you want to achieve, not what you want to avoid. Instead of saying, "I am not bad at math," say, "I am capable and skilled in math."

3. Be Specific:

The more specific the affirmation, the better. "I solve math problems easily and accurately" is more effective than a general statement like "I am good at math."

4. Keep It Simple:

Affirmations should be short and easy to remember. This makes it easier to repeat them regularly.

5. Make It Personal:

Use "I" statements to make affirmations personal and direct. This helps internalize the message more effectively.

Examples of Math-Related Affirmations

Here are some examples of affirmations that XII students can use to develop a love for math:

1. "I enjoy solving math problems and find them interest-

ing."

2. "I am confident in my math skills and abilities."

3. "Math concepts come easily to me."

4. "I am improving in math every day with practice."

5. "I approach math problems with curiosity and enthusiasm."

6. "I am capable of understanding and mastering complex math topics."

7. "Math challenges help me grow and learn."

8. "I believe in my ability to excel in math."

9. "Every math problem has a solution, and I can find it."

10. "I am dedicated to improving my math skills."

How to Incorporate Affirmations into Daily Routine

1. Morning Routine:

Start the day with affirmations. Spend a few minutes each morning repeating your math-related affirmations. This sets a positive tone for the day.

2. Before Study Sessions:

Use affirmations to prepare your mind for math study sessions. This helps create a focused and confident mindset.

3. During Breaks:

Take short breaks during study sessions to repeat affirmations. This can help maintain a positive attitude and reduce stress.

4. Before Exams:

Recite affirmations before taking math exams. This can help calm nerves and boost confidence.

5. Visualization:

Combine affirmations with visualization techniques. Imagine yourself successfully solving math problems and enjoying the process.

6. Written Affirmations:

Write down affirmations and place them where you can see them regularly, such as on your desk, notebook, or mirror.

7. Affirmation Apps:

Use apps designed for affirmations that send daily reminders and help you keep track of your progress.

The transformative power of affirmations in the life of Dr. A.P.J. Abdul Kalam

Dr. A.P.J. Abdul Kalam, one of India's most revered scientists and the 11th President of India, is a prime example of someone who used positive affirmations and a resilient mindset to overcome obstacles and significantly improve his quality of life. His journey from a humble background to becoming the "Missile Man of India" and a beloved leader showcases the power of positive thinking and perseverance.

Early Life and Challenges

Born on October 15, 1931, in Rameswaram, Tamil Nadu, Abdul Kalam hailed from a modest background. His father was a boat owner, and his mother a housewife. Despite financial constraints, his parents encouraged education and hard work. Young Kalam was deeply influenced by his father's strong sense of wisdom and honesty.

From an early age, Kalam faced several hardships. He sold newspapers to supplement his family's income and was often studied by the dim light of oil lamps. However, his determination to pursue education never wavered. He was particularly interested in science and mathematics, subjects that he later excelled in.

Affirmations and Positive Thinking

Kalam's life is a testament to the power of positive affirmations and an unwavering belief in oneself. Throughout his autobiography, "Wings of Fire," he emphasizes the importance of having a positive mindset and the influence of affirmations in his journey. Here are a few instances where affirmations played a crucial role in his life:

1. Educational Pursuits:

Despite failing to achieve his dream of becoming a fighter pilot, Kalam did not let this setback deter him. He affirmed his belief in his ability to succeed in other ways. He said to himself, "I will not give up. I will find another way to serve my country."

2. Facing Professional Challenges:

As a young scientist at the Indian Space Research Organisation (ISRO), Kalam faced numerous challenges. Projects were delayed, and failures were common. Instead of being disheartened, Kalam used affirmations to stay motivated. He often reminded himself, "Success follows persistent efforts and dedication."

3. Leadership and Vision:

As the leader of various missile development programs in India, Kalam encountered significant technical and administrative hurdles. His positive affirmations included, "We can achieve our goals if we stay united and focused."

Key Affirmations in Kalam's Life

Throughout his life, Kalam's use of positive affirmations can be seen in various forms:

1. Belief in Hard Work:

Kalam consistently emphasized the importance of hard work and perseverance. His affirmation, "Dreams are not those which come while we are sleeping, but those when you don't sleep before fulfilling them," inspired countless individuals to pursue their dreams relentlessly.

2. Optimism in Adversity:

Kalam faced several professional setbacks, but he maintained an optimistic outlook. His affirmation, "Man needs his difficulties because they are necessary to enjoy success," highlights his belief in the transformative power of challenges.

3. Faith in Teamwork:

Leading India's missile and space programs required collaboration and teamwork. Kalam's affirmation, "Great dreams of great dreamers are always transcended," reflects his faith in collective effort and vision.

Impact and Legacy

Dr Kalam's use of affirmations and positive thinking not only transformed his own life but also had a profound impact on millions of Indians. As a scientist, he was instrumental in advancing India's space and defence capabilities. As a leader, he inspired a generation to dream big and work hard.

1. Scientific Contributions:

Under his leadership, India saw significant advancements in missile technology and space exploration. Projects like the Agni and Prithvi missiles, and the Pokhran-II nuclear tests, were milestones in India's defence capabilities.

2. Educational Initiatives:

Kalam was passionate about education and youth development. His interactions with students across the country often included affirmations like, "You have to dream before your dreams can come true," encouraging them to pursue their passions.

3. Presidential Tenure:

As President of India from 2002 to 2007, Kalam continued to promote positive thinking and innovation. His presidency was marked by efforts to improve education, technology, and rural development.

Dr A.P.J. Abdul Kalam's life story is a powerful example of how affirmations and a positive mindset can overcome adversity and lead to remarkable achievements. His unwavering belief in hard work, optimism, and teamwork shaped his destiny and inspired millions to believe in their potential. By embracing positive affirmations and maintaining a resilient attitude, Kalam transformed his challenges into opportunities and left a legacy that continues to motivate and inspire.

Affirmations are a powerful tool that can help all students develop a love for math. By reinforcing positive beliefs, shifting mindsets, and reducing anxiety, affirmations can transform how students perceive and engage with math. With regular practice, students can cultivate a positive attitude towards math, leading to improved performance and a lifelong appreciation for the subject.

By integrating affirmations into their daily routine, students can overcome their fears and challenges, unlocking their full potential in mathematics and beyond. Remember, the key to success is believing in yourself and maintaining a positive outlook, and affirmations are a simple yet effective way to achieve that.

Dr A.P.J. Abdul Kalam's life story is a powerful example of how affirmations and a positive mindset can overcome adversity and lead to remarkable achievements. His unwavering belief in hard work, optimism, and teamwork shaped his destiny and inspired millions to believe in their potential. By embracing positive affirmations and maintaining a resilient attitude, Kalam transformed his challenges into opportunities and left a legacy that continues to motivate and inspire.

Affirmations are a powerful tool that can help all students develop a love for math. By reinforcing positive beliefs, shifting mindsets, and reducing anxiety, affirmations can transform how students perceive and engage with math. With regular practice, students can cultivate a positive attitude towards math, leading to improved performance and a lifelong appreciation for the subject.

By integrating affirmations into their daily routine, students can overcome their fears and challenges, unlocking their full potential in mathematics and beyond. Remember, the key to success is believing in yourself and maintaining a positive outlook, and affirmations are a simple yet effective way to achieve that.

It could be something as small as a delicious meal or as big as achieving a goal.

By focusing on the good things, you train your brain to see the world in a more positive light. Whether it's thanking a teacher for their guidance or a friend for their support, expressing gratitude spreads kindness and positivity wherever you go.

Congratulations! You've now unlocked the superpower of gratitude. By practicing gratitude every day, you can make your life brighter, happier, anger-free and more fulfilling. Then, you will be able to learn difficult math concepts easily.

So go ahead, put on your gratitude glasses, and watch the world around you sparkle with positivity and joy!

Activity for reader

Create customized affirmations for yourself.Make yourself ready for abundant blessings of the universe.sample is here for you.

AFFIRMATIONS

- Today is the day I am ready to make it amazing.

- Today is the day I choose to focus on the present moment.

- I am a genius and my mind is working like a Supercomputer.

- I have a sharp and focused memory.

- I am intelligent in Maths and scoring 100% marks.

- I easily understand all the typical logic, concepts, and formulas of Maths.

- I am nourishing my body with healthy choices.

- I am blessed with my loving family.

- I am blessed to be a student of .... School.

- I am performing best in all my subjects.

- I am an achiever, achiever, achiever, achiever, achiever, achiever, achiever.

"If you can change your mind. you can change your life"

– William James

Be the master of your brain

Let you drive your brain, don't let your brain drive you.

You are the master. You are the owner. Have the remote of your brain in your hand. Don't allow your brain to enter any negativity like:

I am weak physically

I am weak mentally

I am not that capable.

I am not worthy.

I am not beautiful

I am not loved etc....

Always be happy, feel joyous, feel good. That's the only thing you have to do. It's only that thing, you get from this book, that you have received the greatest essence of this book. – Rhonda Byrne

So,

Inner happiness actually is the fuel of success.

– Dr. John Hagelin

The knowledge of the secret is being given to you, and what you do with entirely in your hands. Whatever you choose for you is right, whether you choose to use it , or whether you choose not to use it, you get to choose. The freedom of choice is yours.

5 Key Takeaways: Nurture Love for Mathematics

1. Joyful Pursuit: Engage in activities that bring genuine joy and fulfillment.

2. Law of Attraction: Radiate joy to attract positivity, including people, opportunities, and events.

3. Self-Discovery: Ask "What is my joy?" to uncover passions and purpose.

4. Commitment to Joy: Dedicate yourself to joy to amplify its presence in your life.

5. Transformative Power: Embrace joy as a catalyst for personal growth and abundance.

ΛCTIVITY FOR YOU!

Write your customized Habits and Daily Schedule.

____

____

____

____

____

____

____

____

____

REFERENCES

1. Lavretsky, H., et al. (2016). "A Pilot Study of Yogic Meditation for Family

Dementia Caregivers with Depressive Symptoms: Effects on Mental Health,

Cognition, and DNA Methylation. " Journal of Alzheimer's Disease, 52(2),

703-715.

2. Arch, J. J., & Craske, M. G. (2006). "Mechanisms of Mindfulness: Emotion

Regulation Following a Focused Breathing Induction." Emotion, 6(1), 94-107.

3. Brown, R. P., & Gerbarg, P. L. (2009). "Yoga Breathing, Meditation, and

Longevity." Annals of the New York Academy of Sciences, 1172(1), 54-62.

4. Telles, S., et al. (2013). "Immediate Effect of Yoga Breathing with Intermittent

Breath Holding on Reaction Time and Performance in a Stroop Task."

International Journal of Yoga, 6(2), 103-105.

5. Lazar, S. W., et al. (2005). "Meditation Experience is Associated with

Increased Cortical Thickness." NeuroReport, 16(17), 1893-1897.

Books Referred

1. 5 AM Club – Robin Sharma

2. Mindset – Dr. Carol S. Dweck

3. The Power of Now – Eckhart Tolle

4. The Secret – Rhonda Byrne

5. 7 Habits of Highly Effective People – Stephen R. Covey

TESTIMONIALS

Presenting testimonials from past students who not only overcame their fear of math but excelled throughout the entire academic year. I am deeply grateful to have had such dedicated students who wholeheartedly followed my instructions, suggestions, and guidance. I also express my gratitude to the divine powers for blessing me with the wisdom and ability to guide the coming generation effectively.

1. Ashmit Gupta

As a former student of Ms. Laxmi Mittal, I have experienced a monumental impact of her unique teaching methods, which wonderfully explained even some tough concepts of Mathematics in a thoughtfully easy manner. There existed a deep sense of positivity in how she entered the class every time and motivated us not to be scared about Mathematics, but to have a calm head while studying. One particular lesson stands out vividly in my memory. It was one of the days when she demonstrated a fundamental yet unnoticed thing we students often overlooked. Deep breathing, or breathing to the full capacity of our body. She used to say that this oxygen is a key fuel for our bodies and minds to do any task to the best of our potential. Yet, as she pointed out, we seldom breathed as deeply as we should.

Laxmi Ma'am never took mathematics as a monstrous subject as others did and always made learning interesting. I still remember the Monday mornings when we had the first class with her and every week she had something valuable to impart to us, not only related to the subject but how to deal with life positively. I hope all students listen to her valuable insights and try to apply them in their lives for great results.

Ashmit Gupta - Batch 2023
B.A. Honours Economics
Sri Guru Gobind Singh college of commerce
University of Delhi

2. Khushi Sharma

Dear Laxmi Mittal Ma'am,
Congratulations on the publication of your new book! Your calm and compassionate teaching transformed my experience with mathematics. Initially, I was intimidated by the subject, but your patient guidance and encouragement to embrace positive thoughts and beliefs helped me overcome my fears. Because of your dedication, I achieved an impressive 95 marks in my 12th-grade CBSE board exams. Your ability to simplify complex concepts, your unwavering belief in my potential, and your emphasis on forgiveness and positivity made all the difference. Thank you for being an extraordinary teacher and for making a significant impact on my academic journey.

Khushi Sharma
BCA
Asian School of Business, Noida
Batch-2022-2023

3. Vidhi Gupta

Concept clarity is the foundation of every subject, but a great teacher focuses on the overall development of their students. Laxmi Ma'am not only made mathematics understandable through various examples but also provided exercises that helped us stay focused and motivated throughout our journey. The affirmations she encouraged instilled hope within us and kept us motivated, reinforcing the belief that our dreams would one day come true. Additionally, the super brain exercises were highly effective in improving our mental health. Lastly, marking important points and questions from the beginning proved invaluable during revision.

Vidhi Gupta - 98.6% (Class 12) - Delhi Topper

4. Hridya Sharma

Laxmi Ma'am's teaching style is both enlightening and empowering. Her descriptive approach not only clarifies complex mathematical theories but also incorporates affirmations and super brain exercises that stimulate critical thinking and enhance learning retention. Her dedication to ensuring that every student comprehends each topic is evident through her interactive teaching methods, such as practically showcasing a 3-dimensional surface. She creates a supportive classroom atmosphere where students feel encouraged to participate actively and ask questions. She is our insightful guide in mathematics.

Thanks to Laxmi Ma'am, I scored 95 in my 12th board exams despite losing hope of doing well in math. Her unwavering faith in me and refusal to look down on me made all the difference. Her enrichment through affirmations and super brain exercises has proven to be an invaluable resource for all of us.

Hridya Sharma - XII Batch 2023-2024

DISCLAIMER

This book is for educational purposes only. Readers acknowledge that the author does not render legal, financial, medical, or professional advice. The content within this book has been derived from various sources. Please consult a licensed professional before attempting any techniques outlined in this book.

By reading this document, the reader agrees that under no circumstances is the author responsible for any direct or indirect losses incurred as a result of the use of the information contained within this document, including but not limited to errors, omissions, or inaccuracies.

Adherence to all applicable laws and regulations, including international, federal, state, and local governing professional licensing, business practices, advertising, and all other jurisdictions, is the sole responsibility of the purchaser or reader.

Neither the author nor the publisher assumes any responsibility or liability whatsoever on behalf of the purchaser or reader of these materials. Any perceived slight of any individual or organization is purely unintentional.

139